MIGHTY SALADS

FOOD52

MIGHTY SALADS

60 NEW WAYS TO TURN SALAD INTO DINNER—AND MAKE-AHEAD LUNCHES, TOO

Editors of Food52

Photography by James Ransom

TEN SPEED PRESS
California | New York

Contents

PASTA & BREAD SALADS

FISH & SEAFOOD SALADS

MEAT SALADS

Foreword

Lunchtime in our office typically resembles a salad buffet. Some bring ready-to-eat grain or bean salads, assembled over the weekend using components that will maintain their luster for several days. Others tote various bits and bobs with them for à la minute construction, which allows for ingredients—like soft young lettuces or thinly sliced prosciutto—that don't hold up for many days. The team that compiled this book—our editorial team, or Team Salad as it's known in the office—has its own particular ritual: Each person brings in whatever odds and ends are in the fridge at home, and then at lunchtime there is a brief frenzy of chopping and shaving and mixing in the staff kitchen before a magnificent salad materializes to be divvied up among the participants.

What have we learned from being bystanders and participants in this daily parade of colors and textures and acids and oils? That there are many ways to make salad a meal.

We started a column on the site back in 2013 called "Not Sad Desk Lunch"; the lunch salad is the embodiment of that movement. And yes, it is a movement—coming soon to a school or office near you. The point is to be thoughtful about lunch. Not to be fussy or take a lot of time with it, but to resist succumbing to the mind-numbing repetition of logging on to a food delivery service or grabbing the same sad sandwich on your way to work every morning.

Salads also make great one-bowl dinners. There's no better solution to getting dinner on the table after a long day than mixing and matching components from your fridge to create a big, fresh salad. And it's one of the best ways to breathe new life into leftovers such as roast chicken or grilled steak or vegetables.

In this book we give you sixty of our favorite salad recipes, but it doesn't stop there. We've also included loads of tips, riffs, variations, and some ideas that we're pretty sure you've never seen before. Grilled cheese croutons (page 127)? Check. Hard-boiled egg as dressing component (page 14)? Why not? Rice Krispies for crunch (page 139)? Yep, we went there.

We hope you enjoy these mighty salads as much as we do. Here's to fewer sad desk lunches for all!

—Amanda Hesser & Merrill Stubbs, founders of Food52

Introduction

Does anyone need a recipe to make a salad?

That's a great question—and one to which we say no, but also *yes*.

Because although greens + dressing + (maybe) other stuff = salad, that does not a meal make. A salad is the most humble of foods, but also one that can rise, mightily, to main course status. With the right host of elements, a salad can make you feel good *and* fill you up.

The recipes I and the other editors at Food52 compiled in this book will get you there: You'll find salads with parts that are roasted, toasted, frittered, fried, slivered, shaved, marinated, wilted, charred, crisped, and so on. It's salad at its fullest potential.

Half of the dishes in this book are greatest hits from our Food52 community— think grilled peach and apricot salad with kale and prosciutto (page 3) or roasted chickpea salad with za'atar (page 78). They have shown us all the things salad can be. The other half are new creations from Emily Connor, an environmental scientist living in Arlington, Virginia, by way of the Midwest. Under the Food52 name EmilyC, she's posted more than 100 recipes on Food52—and many of them are among our community's most loved (check out that warm bacon vinaigrette on page 105).

Try one of Emily's recipes and you'll ask yourself, "How does she think of this stuff?" and then, "Why have I never done this before?" That's because Emily is fastidious in her researching and tinkering. She finds inspiration from chefs, blogs, and cookbooks and then iterates and riffs until she comes upon a recipe that's comforting, but with so many twists.

She combines ingredients you love but never thought would be good together (cheddar meets grapes on page 135); takes one vegetable and makes it into a full salad (fennel—three ways!—page 81); marinates summer squash in mayonnaise (page 93); and isn't afraid of a wilted green (trust us, page 26). Her salad recipes have made us rethink what a salad can be and are, plainly, so good.

While Emily's and the other recipes in this book are mighty, they are just the beginning. Even if you never make a single recipe in the book to completion but instead create a mash-up you like better or that serves as a happy home for your leftover vegetables, we've done our job.

To get you on your way, we've filled the book with tips and riffs and unscientific formulas. Each recipe is broken down into loose equations so that you can follow along, improvising with your ingredients of choice, and know you'll still end up with a good meal.

We've also included some ideas from food luminaries we turn to for inspiration. These Genius Tips are inspired by the series and book *Genius Recipes*, in which Food52 creative director Kristen Miglore unearths recipes that debunk cooking tropes, help us rethink the way we cook, and solve kitchen problems. Did you know you can pickle chorizo (page 124)—and grains (page 57)? Some geniuses did, and now you do, too.

Salads are a place to play—to use up vegetables, sure, but also to have fun in the kitchen without fear of messing up. They're amenable to another dollop of this or a sprinkle of that, to being eaten from bowls on the couch or elegantly arranged on platters, and even to hanging out in the fridge for the ideal make-ahead lunch or dinner. It's our hope that, with this mighty little book, you'll be doing a lot more of all of this.

—Ali Slagle, books editor of Food52

Building Blocks

All through the book are tips and twists to up your salad situation. We've listed them—and all the dressings—for you here so you can hop to them straightaway.

DRESS WELL

TO GARNISH

Leafy Salads

Grilled Peach & Apricot Salad with Kale and Prosciutto

Sturdy greens + cured meat + grilled fruit + crumbly cheese

Serves 4 | From Nicholas Day

1 bunch lacinato kale

Kosher salt

¼ cup (60ml) olive oil

1 to 2 tablespoons freshly squeezed lemon juice, or to taste

4 ounces (115g) prosciutto, thinly sliced

4 peaches, halved

4 apricots, halved

Neutral oil (such as vegetable, canola, or grapeseed), for brushing

¼ cup (40g) crumbled feta cheese

Crusty bread, for serving

You might think this dressing sounds overly simplified (olive oil and lemon? Why do I need a recipe for that?), but the genius comes when you top the salad with smoky, sweet, still-hot grilled stone fruit. Its juices seep down into the greens and finish what little work you put into the dressing. Add a bit of prosciutto and a tumble of feta, and you've basically got a cheese plate in a bowl. Which, really, is what you wanted from a salad cookbook, right?

1. Heat the grill to medium-high and brush your grates clean. While the grill heats up, prepare the kale. Fold a leaf in half along the central rib. With a sharp knife, cut away the rib and discard. Tear or chop the kale leaves into bite-size pieces and place them in a large salad bowl. Add a pinch of salt and 1 tablespoon of the olive oil and massage, kneading it for a minute or so, until it softens. Whisk together the remaining 3 tablespoons of olive oil and the lemon juice. Tear or cut the prosciutto into bite-size pieces and set both aside.

2. When the grill is reasonably but not overwhelmingly hot, brush the peaches and apricots very lightly with the neutral oil and grill, cut side down, until deeply caramelized, about 5 minutes. Transfer to a plate.

3. Toss the kale with the dressing and feta. Add the prosciutto, followed by the still-hot peaches and apricots, letting their juices seep into the kale. If there are any extra juices on the plate, add those too. Eat with crusty bread.

Genius Tip: Melty Cheese Dressing

You're used to finding hard cheese in crags or pebbles here and there in your salad, but they can also become a more even, consistent coat by melting the cheese into a dressing. Canal House's method starts like you're making cacio e pepe pasta and ends with a milky, emulsified, deeply pungent dressing. Stir 1½ cups (150g) finely grated Pecorino Romano or Parmesan cheese and ½ cup (120ml) boiling water in a large bowl until the cheese is melted. Whisk in ½ cup (120ml) extra-virgin olive oil, then season with freshly ground black pepper. Spoon the melty cheese dressing over skinny asparagus, fresh peas, and delicate lettuce leaves, if you're Canal House—also over heartier greens, roasted vegetables, or scrambled eggs, if you're us.

Petits Pois à la Française Redux

Charred greens + charred alliums + bacon + creamy dressing

Serves 4 | From Aleksandra Mojsilovic

6 ounces (170g) thick-cut bacon

1 teaspoon light brown sugar

¼ teaspoon paprika

20 scallions

3 romaine lettuce hearts

10 ounces (285g) fresh green peas

2 tablespoons extra-virgin olive oil, plus more for brushing

Kosher salt and freshly ground black pepper

Crème Fraîche Dressing

2 tablespoons mayonnaise

2 tablespoons crème fraîche or sour cream

2 tablespoons buttermilk

2 teaspoons freshly squeezed lemon juice

Kosher salt and freshly ground black pepper

Petits pois à la française is classically a simple braise of peas, lettuce, and onions. But Aleksandra Mojsilovic, a scientist by day and James Beard Award–nominated blogger by night, zhooshed it into this, a salad other salads aspire to be: understated at first but full of splendor and temptation. Charred lettuce, peas, and scallions. Caramelized bacon. A luxurious dressing of crème fraîche, buttermilk, mayonnaise, and lemon. You could serve the scallions and lettuce whole for cutting at the table and add some soft-boiled eggs (page 40). Any which way, you'll also want a glass of Chenin Blanc and the sun, setting.

1. Heat the oven to 350°F (175°C). Arrange the bacon slices in a single layer on a baking sheet, then sprinkle with sugar and paprika. Bake until caramelized, about 25 minutes. Let cool on the baking sheet, then cut into ½-inch (1.3cm) pieces.

2. To make the dressing, stir together all the dressing ingredients in a small bowl. Season with salt and pepper.

3. Rinse the scallions and romaine and pat dry. Discard the outer romaine leaves. Cut the romaine hearts in half lengthwise, if you like, keeping the roots intact so they hold together.

4. Heat the broiler with an oven rack 4 to 5 inches (10 to 13cm) from the flame.

5. Spread the peas in a single layer on a large rimmed baking sheet. Toss with the olive oil and season with salt and pepper. Broil, stirring occasionally, until the peas are lightly browned, about 8 minutes. Transfer the peas to a small bowl.

6. Arrange the scallions in a single layer on the same baking sheet. Lightly brush with olive oil, season with salt, and broil until lightly charred, 4 to 5 minutes. Transfer the scallions to a cutting board and let cool for 2 to 3 minutes. Cut the scallions into ¾-inch (2cm) segments.

7. Arrange the romaine in a single layer on the same baking sheet. Lightly brush with olive oil, season with salt and pepper, and broil, turning occasionally, until lightly browned in spots, about 5 minutes. Transfer the romaine to a cutting board and let cool for a few minutes. Cut the romaine into 1-inch (2.5cm) strips. Discard the romaine roots.

8. In a large bowl, toss together the peas, scallions, romaine, and bacon. Add the dressing and toss to coat. Serve immediately.

Featherweight Slaw

Shredded crisp greens + chicken + mayo + nuts/seeds/herbs

Serves 4 | From Amanda Hesser

8 cups (560g) very thinly sliced napa cabbage (about 1 head)

7 ounces (200g) leftover cooked chicken, shredded

½ cup (45g) sliced almonds, toasted

1½ tablespoons sesame seeds, toasted

3 tablespoons fresh basil leaves, thinly sliced or torn

3 scallions, white and light green parts, thinly sliced

Creamy Ginger Dressing

2 tablespoons freshly squeezed lemon juice

2 tablespoons mayonnaise

1 teaspoon peeled, grated fresh ginger

Kosher salt

4 to 5 tablespoons extra-virgin olive oil

We often think that to get slaw cooler, crisper, and lighter, the mayo needs to go. But why take out all the joy? Instead lighten the salad by replacing sturdy wintertime cabbage with featherweight napa. Shredded chicken fits right in, sliced almonds and sesame seeds add a little crunch, and ginger brightens up the dressing. If you'd rather steer the flavors in another direction, go for it, but whatever you do, don't be shy about the mayonnaise. Add as much as you like, you crazy cat.

1. In a large bowl, toss together the cabbage, chicken, almonds, sesame seeds, basil, and scallions.

2. To make the dressing, in a separate bowl, whisk together the lemon juice, mayonnaise, and ginger. Season with salt. Gradually whisk in the olive oil until smooth.

3. Pour most but not all of the dressing over the cabbage mixture and toss until lightly coated. Taste and add more dressing or salt as needed. Feel free to add more oil or mayo if desired. Eat soon—the cabbage gets watery as it wilts.

Lettuces That Last for Weeks

No scary chemicals or Frankenstein foods here—promise. Just wash and spin your lettuces as you normally would, then stick the whole contraption in the fridge, lid and all, and both your hearty and delicate greens can last for weeks. It turns out that there's enough water at the bottom of the bowl to keep the greens from falling limp but not enough to make them spoil. Our creative director, Kristen Miglore, swears by this method—she's had arugula and spinach leaves last for up to a month!

Antipasto Chopped Salad

Lettuce(s) + pickled somethings + meat + cheese

Serves 4 | From Emily Connor

1 small or ½ large red onion, sliced paper-thin

6 tablespoons (90ml) apple cider vinegar

1 tablespoon sugar

1½ teaspoons kosher salt, plus more as needed

1 (15-ounce/425g) can cannellini beans, drained and rinsed

2 cups (300g) cherry tomatoes, halved

1 head radicchio, halved, cored, and cut into ribbons

2 romaine hearts, trimmed and cut into ribbons

5 radishes, trimmed and sliced paper-thin

5 ounces (140g) salami log, peeled and cut into matchsticks

5 ounces (140g) provolone, cut into matchsticks

Artichoke-Dill Dressing

1 (6-ounce/170g) jar marinated artichoke hearts

6 tablespoons (90ml) extra-virgin olive oil

Grated zest of 1 lemon

3 tablespoons freshly squeezed lemon juice

1 teaspoon Dijon mustard

Kosher salt and freshly ground black pepper

3 tablespoons finely chopped fresh dill

The guiding concept of Emily's chopped salad is simple: Toss the ingredients you'd find on an antipasto platter with a bunch of lettuce and dress them. It practically begs for improvisation—add peperoncini, marinated mushrooms, olives, the kitchen sink! But there's one thing we wouldn't touch: the crazy good artichoke-dill dressing, which gets its creaminess (and addictive brininess) from marinated artichoke hearts, no dairy required. Bet you didn't expect an antipasto platter that's good enough to drink.

1. In a microwave-safe container, combine the onion, vinegar, 3 tablespoons water, sugar, and salt. Microwave for 1 minute, then stir and microwave for another minute. Stir in the cannellini beans and let marinate while you prepare the rest of the salad. (To make in advance, marinate the onions and beans for no more than an hour, drain, and refrigerate.)

2. Season the tomatoes with salt.

3. To make the dressing, using a stand or immersion blender, blend the artichokes, olive oil, lemon zest and juice, and mustard until smooth and emulsified. Season with salt and pepper to taste. Stir in the dill.

4. In a large bowl, toss together the radicchio, romaine, tomatoes, radishes, salami, and provolone. Drain the onions and beans, add to the bowl, and toss. Add the dressing, a little at a time, tossing to evenly coat. Serve right away.

Lettuce Switcheroo

Let your greens go wild, swapping them in and out of salads with abandon—but also reason. Consider the green's structure and pick an alternate in the same category: Delicate greens include arugula, watercress, mizuna, and baby spinach. Crisp-tender ones are Bibb, Little Gem, and romaine. Sturdy fellows include radicchio, kale, collards, and chard.

Happy, Healthy Herbs

Sayonara, Herb Stems

While plucking leaves one by one might be your best option for herbs with big leaves, like basil and mint, for the others, there are more efficient ways. For cilantro, parsley, or dill, grab your bunch by the stems. Hold it up so the leaves are just skimming the cutting board. Working away from you, toward the leaves, move your knife down the stems, removing the leaves as if you were peeling a vegetable. You'll end up with a pile of leaves, and maybe some tender stems, in no time. For heartier herbs like thyme or rosemary, reverse it. Hold the top of the plant and, working away from you, pinch the stem with your fingers and move your way down to where the root was, detaching the leaves from the stem.

How to Fry Herbs

If you've already dirtied a pan, or—better—have a pan with a puddle of oil, you can fry sturdy herbs for a garnish. In a matter of seconds, they transform into papery wisps ready to dance atop your salads—or crostini, pasta, or tacos. Parsley, sage, and rosemary work well, but mint and basil discolor. In a pot or sauté pan with a lid, heat ½ inch (1.3cm) of vegetable oil over medium-high heat until shimmering. Add the really dry herb leaves to the hot oil and cover the pan immediately to avoid splattering. Fry until crisp. For parsley and rosemary, about 15 seconds, while sage takes closer to 45 seconds. Watch the leaves as they can burn quickly. Using a slotted spoon or tongs, transfer the fried leaves to a paper towel–lined plate. Season with kosher salt. Use immediately.

The Best Way to Store Herbs

Bunches of soft fresh herbs (think basil, parsley, cilantro, and tarragon) resemble flower bouquets and should be stored as such: upright in a jar with water, which should be changed every day or two. Basil can stay on the counter, all the better to admire it, while the others go in the fridge (covered with a plastic bag if you're very protective). To store hard-stemmed herbs like rosemary, thyme, marjoram, and oregano, just wrap them in a wet paper towel or kitchen towel, then cover in plastic wrap or put in a plastic container before refrigerating. Herbs will keep for up to 2 weeks.

How to Revive Wilty Vegetables & Herbs

Squishy Beet, Droopy Cilantro, and Limp Carrot have been hanging around the bottom of your crisper for some time now (weeks?). They're getting wiltier by the day as you're feeling guiltier; but instead of composting them, throw them a life vest. Vegetables go limp because they're dehydrated; they lose water as time goes on, causing them to forgo their turgidity and crispness. To perk up your vegetables and herbs, then, let them drink. Plunk them in a bowl of cold or room-temperature water, then refrigerate them. Depending on limpness and plant type, the specimen could be revived from anywhere between 15 minutes (celery) and 1 hour (peeled potatoes). We've had good results with root vegetables, plants with porous outsides (such as celery and rhubarb), and soft herbs like parsley, cilantro, and basil.

Turn Any Pesto into Dressing

With herby pesto around, you're halfway to a cure-all for sad salads. Take Food52 contributor Phyllis Grant's lead: She adds 2 tablespoons olive oil and 2 teaspoons white wine vinegar or Champagne vinegar to every ¼ cup (60ml) pesto—store-bought or homemade (page 86). Whisk and you have dressing. Add freshly squeezed lemon juice and salt till it tastes even better. If it's too thin, add more pesto; too thick, add more oil.

Hoppin' John Salad with Crispy Cornbread

Sturdy greens + toasty bread + bacony beans and vegetables

Serves 4 | From Emily Connor

1½ pounds (680g) collard greens

2 tablespoons apple cider vinegar

1 teaspoon honey

5 ounces (140g) day-old cornbread

1 tablespoon olive oil

4 slices thick-cut bacon, finely diced

2 tablespoons unsalted butter

¼ teaspoon red pepper flakes

1 red bell pepper, seeded and finely diced

5 scallions, white and light green parts, thinly sliced

2 teaspoons finely chopped fresh thyme

1½ cups (250g) cooked black-eyed peas

Kosher salt and freshly ground black pepper

This salad is comforting in ways they often aren't: humble in its list of ingredients, warmed through, spiced, smoky, and fortifying. Its components can be prepped days in advance and then assembled on the fly. The ingredients are also amenable to swaps: chard for collards, cannellini beans for black-eyed peas, ciabatta for cornbread, pancetta for bacon.

1. Fold each collard leaf in half along the central rib. With a sharp knife, cut away the rib and discard. Stack a few of the leaves on top of each other, roll them like a cigar, and cut crosswise into ⅛-inch (3mm) ribbons. Repeat until all of the leaves are shredded.

2. In a small bowl, whisk together the vinegar and honey. Tear the cornbread into ½-inch (1.3cm) pieces—they don't have to be perfect!

3. In a 12-inch (30cm) skillet or sauté pan over medium heat, warm the olive oil. Add the bacon and cook, stirring every so often, until the fat renders and the bacon is lightly crisp, 10 to 15 minutes. Transfer the bacon to a paper towel–lined plate. Pour the bacon fat into a small, heatproof bowl. Wipe out the pan.

4. Return 2 tablespoons of the bacon fat to the pan and warm over medium-high heat until it shimmers. Add the cornbread crumbs and cook, stirring frequently, until most of the pieces are dark golden brown and crispy, 3 to 6 minutes. Transfer the cornbread to a bowl. Wipe out the pan.

5. Pour 1 tablespoon of the bacon fat into the pan, add the butter, and warm over medium heat. When the butter melts and sizzles, add the red pepper flakes and cook until lightly toasted, about 20 seconds. Add the bell pepper, scallions, thyme, black-eyed peas, and a pinch of salt and sauté until the bell pepper is crisp-tender, 3 to 4 minutes. Working in batches if necessary, add the collards, a pinch of salt, and a pinch of pepper and toss until the collards are evenly coated with the bacon fat and butter. Continue to sauté just until the collards begin to wilt and turn bright green and glossy, about 2 minutes.

6. Off the heat, return any collards you've set aside to the pan, then add the vinegar-honey mixture and toss. Taste and adjust the seasoning. Add the bacon and toss. Transfer to a platter, scatter the cornbread over the top, and serve immediately.

Cobb Salad with Hard-Boiled Egg Dressing

Lettuces + rows of protein, vegetables, and fun stuff + herbs + creamy dressing

Serves 4 | From Emily Connor

¼ cup (60ml) white wine vinegar

Kosher salt

4 large red beets, scrubbed well, trimmed, and halved

1 large head Bibb lettuce, torn into large pieces

⅓ cup (15g) loosely packed fresh tarragon, dill, or chives, coarsely chopped

4 hard-cooked eggs (page 62), quartered

1 large avocado, peeled, pitted, and thinly sliced

⅓ cup (45g) Niçoise olives, pitted

½ cup (70g) crumbled blue cheese

Hard-Boiled Egg Dressing

6 tablespoons (90ml) extra-virgin olive oil

1 hard-boiled egg plus 1 hard-boiled yolk

Grated zest of 1 lemon

3 tablespoons freshly squeezed lemon juice

1 tablespoon capers

2 teaspoons Dijon mustard

Kosher salt

Red pepper flakes

Like many things, cooking is more fun when you break the rules. This dish is our case in point: Why should you have to make Cobb salad the usual way? Why *wouldn't* you add steamed beets or oily black olives? The same goes for the dressing. Why only top your Cobb with hard-boiled eggs when you can blend them into a dressing that's creamy without any dairy (similar to a quick sauce gribiche)? It's all a little rebellious, but still a Cobb, no doubt. Feel better now?

1. In a large saucepan, bring 2 inches (5cm) of water, the vinegar, and several pinches of kosher salt to a boil over high heat. Put the beets in a steamer basket and set the basket over the boiling water. Cover the pan, turn the heat to medium, and steam until the beets are tender when pierced with a knife, about 20 minutes. Let cool, then peel and cut into bite-size pieces.

2. To make the dressing, using a stand or immersion blender, blend all of the ingredients together until smooth and emulsified. Add salt and pepper flakes to taste.

3. On a large platter or wide bowl, toss together the lettuce with half of the herbs. Add enough dressing to lightly coat the leaves, and toss again. Arrange the beets, eggs, avocado, olives, and cheese in rows on top. Scatter the remaining herbs. (You can also toss everything together.) Serve with the remaining dressing on the side.

Keep an Avocado from Browning

To stop your avocado from browning, the lazy way also happens to be the best way. Our senior staff writer, Sarah Jampel, put various methods to the test: sticking avocado halves in sealed containers with red onion, lemon juice, olive oil, coconut oil, or cold water; boiling and shocking; and storing them on their own, with and without the pit. After 24 hours, most "preventative measures" did more harm than good, and the avocados in the best condition were the ones that asked the least of us—the half with the pit looked greenest, and the one without was the runner-up.

Caesar-Style Kale Salad with Roasted Onions

Hearty greens + roasted alliums + umami flavor bombs + Caesar-like dressing

Serves 4 | From Paula Marchese

2 yellow onions, sliced into ¼-inch (6mm) half-moons

2 thyme sprigs

1 rosemary sprig

3½ tablespoons extra-virgin olive oil

Kosher salt and freshly ground black pepper

3 slices day-old ciabatta or sourdough, cubed

1 small bunch lacinato kale

4 slices thick-cut bacon, sliced into 1-inch (2.5cm) pieces

1 (15-ounce/425g) can cannellini beans, drained and rinsed

1 cup grated ricotta salata (240g) or crumbled feta (150g)

Caesar Dressing

1½ tablespoons freshly squeezed lemon juice

1½ teaspoons rice vinegar

12 capers, coarsely chopped

1 or 2 large anchovy fillets, coarsely chopped

1 teaspoon Dijon mustard

½ teaspoon Worcestershire sauce

¼ cup (60ml) extra-virgin olive oil

Kosher salt and freshly ground black pepper

Don't resist the "kaleification" of the Caesar salad—it's objectively delicious and spares romaine the avalanche of dressing that's too heavy for its ridges. But this isn't just any kale Caesar. It's bold with umami, what with the ricotta salata, bacon, capers, *and* anchovies. And the roasted onion half-moons—neither stiffly raw nor caramelized to oblivion—are good here and also everywhere. Go ahead, make an extra batch.

1. Heat the oven to 350°F (175°C). Arrange the onions, thyme, and rosemary in a single layer on a rimmed baking sheet. Toss with 2 tablespoons of the olive oil until evenly coated. Season with ¼ teaspoon salt and a pinch of pepper and toss again. Roast until the onions turn golden but aren't charred, 60 to 75 minutes.

2. In a large heavy pan, warm the remaining 1½ tablespoons of olive oil over low heat. Add the bread cubes and cook, turning occasionally, until toasted and golden on all sides, about 10 minutes. Transfer the croutons to a paper towel–lined plate and sprinkle with salt.

3. To make the dressing, using a stand or immersion blender, blend the lemon juice, rice vinegar, capers, anchovies, mustard, and Worcestershire sauce until smooth. With the blender running, pour the olive oil in a thin stream and blend until thoroughly emulsified. Taste and adjust the salt, pepper, and lemon; the dressing should taste vibrant and lemony. (The dressing will keep in a glass jar in the fridge for up to 3 days. Bring to room temp before using.)

4. Fold each kale leaf in half along the central rib. With a sharp knife, cut away the rib and discard. Stack a few of the leaves on top of each other, roll them like a cigar, and cut crosswise into ⅛-inch (3mm) ribbons. Put the kale in a serving bowl, add three-quarters of the dressing, and toss until the leaves are evenly coated.

5. Heat a small skillet over medium heat. Cook the bacon, stirring every so often, until crunchy, about 5 minutes. With a slotted spoon, put the bacon on top of the kale (add a little of the rendered fat, too, if you like).

6. Add the onions and their juices to the kale and toss with your hands or tongs. Add the croutons, beans, and ricotta salata. Taste and adjust the seasoning, adding more dressing if the salad's dry.

Radicchio & Cauliflower
with Currant-Anchovy Vinaigrette

Bitter greens + brassica + legumes + nuts/herbs/cheese + gutsy vinaigrette

Serves 4 | From Emily Connor

1 head (about 450g) cauliflower, cut into small florets

3 tablespoons olive oil, plus more as needed

½ teaspoon Aleppo pepper

Kosher salt

1 head radicchio, cored and chopped

½ cup (100g) green lentils, rinsed and picked over

1 bay leaf

½ cup (25g) coarsely chopped fresh tarragon

⅓ cup (40g) coarsely chopped toasted walnuts

3 ounces (85g) fresh or slightly aged goat cheese or feta

Currant-Anchovy Vinaigrette

3 anchovy fillets

5 tablespoons (75ml) extra-virgin olive oil

2 tablespoons minced shallots

2 tablespoons balsamic vinegar

1 teaspoon Dijon mustard

1 tablespoon freshly squeezed lemon juice, plus more as needed

½ teaspoon honey

3 tablespoons currants

This salad has all five basic tastes covered, so it is, by definition of its ingredients, a balanced dish. There's a lot of big flavors—anchovy-soaked cauliflower; bitter radicchio, raw and roasted; salty cheese; sweet currants—so each forkful might be a little different but still harmonious. It's so Zen, you can make it fully dressed a day ahead—just bring it to room temp before serving.

1. Heat the oven to 400°F (200°C). Line a large rimmed baking sheet with parchment paper. Spread the cauliflower into a single layer on the baking sheet. Toss with 2 tablespoons of the olive oil, the Aleppo pepper, and a pinch or two of salt to evenly coat. (Add more oil if needed.) Spread into a single layer again and roast until the cauliflower is light brown, 20 to 25 minutes.

2. Meanwhile, in a separate bowl, toss half of the radicchio with the remaining 1 tablespoon of olive oil. When the cauliflower is light brown, scatter the remaining undressed radicchio on the sheet and roast until the radicchio is wilted and the cauliflower is tender, 3 to 5 minutes more. Let cool.

3. To make the vinaigrette, finely chop the anchovies and smash them into a paste with the side of a chef's knife. Combine with the remaining ingredients and whisk together until emulsified. Add more lemon to taste.

4. Place the lentils, bay leaf, and a few pinches of salt in a saucepan and add enough cold water to cover by at least 1 inch (2.5cm). Bring to a boil, then turn down the heat and simmer until tender, 20 to 25 minutes. Add additional water if needed. Drain well, discard the bay leaf, and transfer to a large bowl. Mix in enough vinaigrette to lightly coat and a few pinches of salt while the lentils are still warm.

5. Toss in the cauliflower, roasted radicchio, raw radicchio, tarragon, and walnuts to the bowl. Toss with more vinaigrette until evenly dressed. Taste and adjust the seasoning, adding more lemon juice if needed. Just before serving, crumble the goat cheese over the salad and gently toss. Serve warm or at room temperature.

Roasted Grape, Butternut Squash & Kale Salad

Roasted winter squash + roasted fruit + hearty greens + hard cheese + cheesy vinaigrette
Serves 4 | From Elizabeth Stark

1/2 teaspoon sea salt

1/4 teaspoon chipotle chile powder

1/4 teaspoon red pepper flakes

Pinch of paprika

Pinch of freshly ground black pepper

1 small butternut squash, peeled, halved lengthwise, seeded, and cut into bite-sized chunks

2 1/2 teaspoons extra-virgin olive oil

2 cups (300g) seedless Concord or red grapes

8 ounces (225g) baby kale leaves

1 ounce (30g) Parmesan, shaved with a vegetable peeler

Parmesan Vinaigrette

1 garlic clove, minced

1 tablespoon sherry vinegar

1 tablespoon Dijon mustard

1 teaspoon honey

1/4 teaspoon paprika

Pinch of sea salt

1/4 cup (60ml) extra-virgin olive oil

2 tablespoons finely grated Parmesan

To make a salad of autumn's all-stars come together as a coherent whole, the blogger behind Brooklyn Supper relies on the same family of ingredients (paprika, chipotle chile powder, and red pepper flakes) to season the roasted squash and grapes *and* the salad dressing. Parmesan cheese, too, does double duty: It's finely shredded and mixed into the dressing and then shaved and strewn across the finished dish. The star, though, is still the admittedly drippy, caramelized grapes, which release their juices and develop an adorably wrinkled skin after just a short run in the oven.

1. Heat the oven to 400°F (200°C). Line two large baking sheets with parchment paper. (If you have a large oven, you can roast everything at once; otherwise, it's best to roast the squash first and then the grapes after.)

2. In a small bowl, combine the salt, chile powder, red pepper flakes, paprika, and black pepper.

3. In a large bowl, toss the butternut squash with 2 teaspoons of the olive oil and three-quarters of the spice mixture. Arrange in a single layer on the prepared baking sheets, leaving plenty of room in between the chunks. (No need to wash the bowl.) Roast for 20 minutes, then flip and continue to roast until the squash is tender and edges are lightly browned, 15 to 20 minutes more. Slide the parchment onto a wire rack to cool (you'll be using one of the baking sheets again).

4. In the same bowl used for the squash, toss the grapes with the remaining 1/2 teaspoon of olive oil and the remaining spice mixture. Arrange the grapes in a single layer on a parchment-lined baking sheet and roast, shaking once or twice, just until the grapes start to burst, 8 to 10 minutes.

5. To make the vinaigrette, whisk together the garlic, vinegar, mustard, honey, paprika, and salt. Gradually whisk in the olive oil until emulsified. Fold in the grated Parmesan.

6. Toss the kale with half of the vinaigrette and arrange on a platter. Tuck the squash chunks and grapes among the kale leaves. Scatter the shaved Parmesan over the top and drizzle with the remaining vinaigrette. Serve warm or at room temperature.

Chard Salad with Garlic Breadcrumbs & Parmesan

Cheese-coated greens + garlicky breadcrumbs + lemon + protein

Serves 2 | From Merrill Stubbs

1 lemon

Kosher salt

½ cup (120ml) extra-virgin olive oil

1½ cups (165g) fresh breadcrumbs

1 garlic clove, minced

1 bunch Swiss chard

¾ cup (75g) finely grated Parmesan

10 slices bresaola, torn into small pieces

½ cup (55g) sliced almonds, toasted

You've probably had a salad with these flavors before. It was likely kale, with croutons and Parmesan as sporadic garnishes. But if you change the coarseness of the bread and add a lot more of it, throw in a bunch more Parmesan, and swap kale for silkier Swiss chard ribbons and its finely chopped stems, you have a salad with textures and flavors that keep your attention for more than two bites. Merrill recreated this salad after having it at a favorite Brooklyn restaurant, Stone Park Cafe. She chops the stems so finely that their raw crunch is pleasing, and the chard ribbons loop around each other like noodles, picking up the heaps of Parmesan and garlicky breadcrumbs with the help of a lemon dressing. Toasted almonds and torn bresaola make it a meal, but so would pistachios, pumpkin seeds, or walnuts; prosciutto, salami, or mortadella; rainbow chard or, sure, lacinato kale instead of (or alongside) the Swiss chard.

1. Juice and zest the lemon. In a small bowl, combine 2½ tablespoons of the lemon juice, 1 teaspoon of the lemon zest, and a few generous pinches of salt. Slowly whisk in ¼ cup (60ml) of the olive oil.

2. In a small, heavy skillet, heat the remaining ¼ cup (60ml) of olive oil over medium heat. Add the breadcrumbs and cook, stirring frequently, until crisp and golden brown, about 5 minutes. Be careful not to burn them! Stir in the garlic and let the breadcrumbs toast for a minute more, then remove from the heat.

3. Separate the chard leaves from their stems and finely chop the stems. Stack a few of the leaves on top of each other, roll them like a cigar, and cut crosswise into ⅛-inch (3mm) ribbons. Repeat until all the leaves are shredded. Put the chard stems and leaves into a large bowl and toss gently with the Parmesan and about two-thirds of the lemon dressing. Taste and add more dressing if you like. Toss in the bresaola, almonds, and toasted breadcrumbs and serve immediately.

How to Save So-So
(& Plain Terrible) Dressing

From Catherine Lamb

The simplest solution for too sweet, too acidic, too salty, or just plain boring dressing happens to come in a rhyme: When in doubt, thin it out. Diluting your dressing by adding more of all the flavors—minus the overwhelming one—will help restore balance. There are specific solutions, too, depending on your dressing's diagnosis.

If your dressing is too sweet

Add something savory. Salt, of course, will work, but if you want something a little more interesting, opt for preserved lemon (page 32), anchovies, capers, soy sauce, or miso. Just make sure you're matching with the flavor profile of your dish. Capers in a peanut dressing? We'd choose soy instead.

If your dressing is too salty

Temper it with something sweet. Sugar works, but your dressing will get some extra oomph from honey, maple syrup, or pomegranate molasses (page 65).

If your dressing is too acidic

Adding something creamy will round it out, but make sure the creaminess fits in with the rest of your dressing. A nut butter like tahini or peanut butter plays well with a soy sauce- or miso-fueled dressing; avocado works well with herbaceous ones; blend in a soft- (page 40) or hard-boiled (page 62) egg if you're feeling bold.

If you want to keep your dressing on a vinaigrette-like path, try adding a bit of red wine—not red wine *vinegar*. Wine will "make up for imperfections in your vinegar," as Molly Wizenberg put it in her memoir *Delancey*. Her husband, Brandon Pettit, came up with this trick when he ran out of his good vinegar. If your vinaigrette is made with white wine vinegar, go for dry bubbly; replace apple cider vinegar with sour beer.

If your salad dressing is a little too one-note

Add some ace-in-the-hole flavor brighteners: herbs, grated cheese, horseradish, chile flakes, and maybe just a little more salt and pepper.

Wilted Escarole with Feta & Honey

Seared greens + cheese + nuts + sweetness

Serves 2 | From Dorie Colangelo

1 head escarole, halved lengthwise with root intact

Kosher salt and freshly ground black pepper

4 teaspoons extra-virgin olive oil

4 ounces (115g) feta, crumbled

32 walnut halves, chopped

Honey, for drizzling

When escarole's toughness is tamed by heat and its bitterness by honey, it can be downright seductive. And when seared escarole is covered in walnuts, feta, and generous drizzles of honey, you have a dish that, according to its creator Dorie Colangelo, meets all the marks of a good salad: salty, crunchy, and creamy, too. For additional heartiness, scatter some roasted shrimp (page 105), crispy chickpeas and salami (page 43), or grilled lamb (page 132) over top.

1. Wash the escarole thoroughly, making sure to get between the leaves to rid them of any sand. Shake off most of the water and sprinkle the escarole with salt and pepper.

2. In a large sauté pan, warm the olive oil over medium-high heat. Place the escarole in the pan and sear until all of the leaves are slightly wilted, 30 to 40 seconds per side.

3. Transfer the escarole to a serving plate and scatter with the feta and walnuts. Drizzle with honey. Serve immediately.

How to Wash Greens

Our way of washing greens isn't revolutionary, but it works quite well. Fill a big bowl with cold water, add the greens, and swish them around. Let them sit for a few minutes so dirt can float to the bottom. Gently remove the leaves from the water, being sure not to drain the water and leaves together, inadvertently showering your just-cleaned greens with dirt. Repeat the process with a fresh bowl of water until the water is mostly clear. Dry the leaves well with a salad spinner or roll them up in a kitchen towel.

Less-Leafy Vegetable Salads

Shaved Asparagus with Burrata, Radish & Cucumber

Thinly sliced veg + alliums + Burrata + acid

Serves 2 | From Aleksandra Mojsilovic

8 ounces (225g) asparagus

6 ounces (170g) radishes, thinly sliced

6 ounces (170g) cucumber, finely diced

4 ounces (115g) Burrata

Microgreens or pea greens, for the top

Crusty bread, for serving

Lime Vinaigrette
1 tablespoon white balsamic vinegar

1 tablespoon freshly squeezed lime juice, plus more as needed

½ teaspoon grated lime zest

5 tablespoons (75ml) extra-virgin olive oil

3 stalks green garlic or ramps, white and light green parts, minced

Sea salt and freshly ground black pepper

The first signs of spring—asparagus, radishes, green garlic—are meant to be savored: Shave them paper-thin so they're on display on the plate, then accompany them with a big puddle of Burrata for a meal-worthy salad. With jewels so bright, you need little else. To carry this salad's elegance into colder months, with a mandoline or stellar knife skills, shave persimmons, brussels sprouts, endive, beets, turnips, kohlrabi, pears, and apples. Swap out young garlic for scallions. Always keep the Burrata, though—the buttery cow's milk cheese never goes out of style.

1. Snap off the tough bottoms of the asparagus and discard. Snap off the tips, then cut them into thin slices. Using a vegetable peeler, shave the spears lengthwise by holding the end with your nondominant hand and peeling away from your hand using even, heavy pressure. You can rest the flat surface you first create on a cutting board for a more stable base as you shave the rest of the spear.

2. To make the vinaigrette, in a small bowl, whisk together the vinegar, lime juice, and lime zest. Gradually whisk in the olive oil until smooth. Stir in the green garlic and season generously with salt and pepper. Taste and adjust the seasoning, adding more lime juice if necessary.

3. Divide the radishes, cucumber, and asparagus between two plates. Dollop the Burrata, drizzle the vinaigrette, and scatter the microgreens. Serve with crusty bread if you like.

Is It a Sprout or a Shoot or a Microgreen?

When you see a little stem coming out of a seed (or bean, grain, or nut) and maybe some root hairs, that's a *sprout*, and the entire thing can be eaten (page 66). But when seeds have grown a little more in soil or another growing medium and start to resemble tiny plants, they're clipped near the base of their stems and called *shoots*. If you're thinking that shoots remind you of microgreens, you're not alone: The term *microgreens* doesn't have a set definition. It's a buzzy marketing word that has been used to refer to greens a little bit further along than sprouts—but also any greens younger than the baby stage. It's all a little confusing, but because you're not usually cooking any of these greens, nothing will go *too* wrong if you don't pick the right one.

Fried Eggplant, Tomato & Peach Salad with Preserved Lemon Vinaigrette

Fried vegetables + crisp fruit + soft cheese + herbs + pungent vinaigrette

Serves 4 | From Emily Connor

¾ cup (175ml) vegetable oil

1 Asian eggplant, cut into ¾-inch (2cm) cubes

Wondra flour, for dusting

Kosher salt

2 Persian cucumbers, cut into ¾-inch (2cm) cubes

2 cups (300g) cherry tomatoes, halved

1 large, ripe peach, pitted and thinly sliced

1 (8-ounce/225g) fresh mozzarella ball, cut into ½-inch (1.3cm) slices

1 cup (20g) loosely packed basil leaves, coarsely chopped or torn

Preserved Lemon Vinaigrette

1 tablespoon chopped preserved lemon rind (page 115)

1 teaspoon freshly squeezed lemon juice, plus more as needed

¼ cup (60ml) extra-virgin olive oil

½ teaspoon piment d'Espelette or Aleppo pepper

Kosher salt (optional)

At its best, fried eggplant has a golden outside and creamy inside, with a chew that relaxes to silkiness. At its worst, it's an oil-thirsty sponge that drinks and drinks while remaining tough and dry. For this salad—where the eggplant needs to justify its existence among the summer's ripest, sweetest fruit—we choose door number one, and a technique for getting fried eggplant right that doesn't involve a long wait time or a deep-fryer. The eggplant is cubed, dusted with Wondra (an "instant flour" that fancy chefs turn to for crispy-coated chicken and fish), and pan-fried until it's a perfect tender-rich foil to all the cucumber, tomato, and peach freshness. You can substitute half all-purpose flour and half cornstarch for the Wondra if you need.

1. In a 12-inch (30cm) skillet, warm the vegetable oil over medium-high heat to 350°F (175°C). Dust the eggplant cubes with Wondra. Working in batches if needed, arrange the eggplant in a single layer and cook, turning a few times, until golden brown and tender, about 3 minutes. Adjust the heat as necessary to keep the oil at 350°F (175°C). Using a slotted spoon, transfer the eggplant to a paper towel–lined plate to drain. Season with salt and let cool.

2. To make the vinaigrette, whisk together the vinaigrette ingredients. Taste and add salt and more lemon juice if needed.

3. In a large bowl, toss together the cucumbers, tomatoes, and peach. Drizzle in half of the vinaigrette and toss to combine. Season with salt. Let sit for a few minutes.

4. Arrange the salad on a large serving platter, then scatter the mozzarella, basil, and eggplant on top. Drizzle with a little more of the vinaigrette so the eggplant is lightly coated. Season with black pepper, and serve immediately.

Corn-Barley Salad with Tomato Vinaigrette

Grilled vegetables + grains + beans + herbs + fruity vinaigrette

Serves 4 | From Jeannine Balletto

½ cup (100g) pearl barley

3 ears fresh juicy corn

¼ to ½ cup (60 to 120ml) olive oil, plus more for grilling

1 super-ripe tomato, halved

1 large garlic clove

Kosher salt

Pinch of crushed red pepper flakes

1½ teaspoons white wine vinegar

2 cups (300g) cherry tomatoes, halved

1 cup (180g) cooked cannellini beans

¼ cup (8g) firmly packed fresh basil, cut into ribbons

1 bunch chives, thinly sliced

Your best fruity olive oil, for drizzling

Tomato water and corn milk may not sound like ingredients you'd be particularly interested in eating, or drinking, but as the base of a vinaigrette, suddenly—magically?—a grain salad that has tomato in it tastes like tomato. And there's corn, too, but the flavor is brighter and quite literally juicier. That "milk" is the sweet, starchy liquid that's scraped from corncobs, while the tomato water is made from the rosy juice and pulp of a grated tomato. While you're adding a few more steps to an otherwise straightforward salad, it now shouts "summer!" so loudly, we can almost smell the tomato vines.

1. Heat a grill or grill pan to medium-high heat. Bring a large stockpot of generously salted water to a boil.

2. Add the barley to the pot and cook it according to the package directions. During the last 5 or 6 minutes of cooking, add the corn.

3. Remove the corn with tongs. Drain the barley and set aside. Brush the corn with olive oil and grill until charred on all sides, about 8 minutes.

4. Cut the kernels from the corncobs (page 110). As you cut the kernels, collect all of the corn milk that drips into a bowl, then use the back of the knife to scrape the remaining corn milk from the cleaned cob.

5. Grate the large tomato on the large holes of a box grater over a wide bowl, collecting the juice and pulp. Discard the tomato skins.

6. Place the garlic on a cutting board, sprinkle with a couple of generous pinches of salt, and finely chop and smash it into a paste with the side of a chef's knife. Add the garlic paste to the tomato pulp, as well as a pinch of salt, the red pepper flakes, vinegar, and reserved corn milk. Gradually whisk in enough of the olive oil until the vinaigrette is emulsified.

7. In a serving bowl, combine the barley, corn, cherry tomatoes, beans, basil, and chives. Add the vinaigrette and toss to evenly coat. Drizzle with fruity olive oil and serve.

Charred Okra Succotash Salad

Charred and raw veg + smoky meat + beans + heat + herbs

Serves 4 | From Emily Connor

1 pound (450g) okra

1 tablespoon olive oil, plus more as needed

4 slices thick-cut bacon, cut crosswise into lardons

2 cups (310g) fresh or frozen lima beans

Kosher salt

4 cups (620g) fresh corn kernels (from 4 ears of corn)

4 scallions, white and light green parts, thinly sliced

¼ teaspoon red pepper flakes

2 cups (300g) cherry tomatoes, halved

Juice of 1 lemon, to taste

¼ cup (8g) firmly packed flat-leaf parsley leaves, torn

¼ cup (8g) firmly packed basil leaves, torn

First, choose small, pinky-size okra so they're soft—even sweet. Blacken them whole *in a slick of bacon fat*, and they're suddenly the smoky, meaty, crunchy backbone that your summer succotash has always longed for. Corn, tomatoes, and limas get tossed right in the same skillet, and the whole dish is finished with bright, punchy hits of lemon, parsley, and basil; it is a salad, after all—a best-of-summer, spoonable, no-slime salad.

1. Rinse and thoroughly dry the okra, then trim the tops.

2. In a 12-inch (30cm) skillet (cast iron works well), heat the olive oil over medium heat. Add the bacon and cook, stirring every so often, until crisp, about 5 minutes. Transfer the bacon to a paper towel–lined plate to drain. Pour the bacon fat into a small, heatproof bowl. Wipe out the pan.

3. Meanwhile, bring a pot of salted water to a boil. Add the lima beans, turn down the heat, and simmer until tender, which can take anywhere from a few minutes to 20 minutes, depending on the freshness of your lima beans. Drain.

4. Coat the bottom of the pan with bacon fat and warm over medium-high heat until it shimmers. Working in batches, arrange the okra in a single layer in the pan, being careful not to crowd them. Season with a few pinches of salt and cook, undisturbed, until nicely charred on the bottom, several minutes. Flip the okra and continue to cook until crisp-tender and charred on all sides, about 3 minutes. Taste an okra pod to check doneness; if the okra is charring too quickly, turn down the heat. Transfer the okra to a paper towel–lined plate to drain.

5. Pour more bacon fat or olive oil into the pan if needed and warm over medium-high heat. Add the corn, scallions, and red pepper flakes and sauté until the corn is crisp-tender, 2 to 3 minutes. Season with salt.

6. Turn the heat to low and add the bacon, lima beans, and cherry tomatoes. Toss gently and cook until just warmed through, about 1 minute. Taste and adjust the seasoning, adding as much of the lemon juice as you like. Remove from the heat.

7. Add the parsley and basil and toss together. Serve warm or at room temperature.

Grilled Mushroom & Fig Salad

Grilled marinated mushrooms + grilled and fresh fruit + spicy greens + crunch

Serves 4 | From Emily Connor

4 portobello mushrooms, stemmed

10 to 12 (about 1 pint) figs (such as Black Mission or Calimyrna), trimmed and halved

6 cups (180g) firmly packed baby arugula leaves

Kosher salt

1 (2-ounce/55g) chunk aged Pecorino Romano, shaved with a vegetable peeler

⅓ cup (50g) Marcona almonds, coarsely chopped

Balsamic-Thyme Vinaigrette

½ cup (120ml) extra-virgin olive oil

3 tablespoons balsamic vinegar

2 tablespoons sherry vinegar

2 tablespoons minced shallots

2 teaspoons finely chopped fresh thyme

1 teaspoon Dijon mustard

¼ teaspoon kosher salt, plus more as needed

Lucky for those of you on whisking or dish-washing duty, this salad is a study in multitasking. The balsamic vinaigrette is not *just* a vinaigrette that'll catch on the arugula, it's also a marinade for mushrooms and figs on their way to the grill. Not only does this streamline your kitchen tasks, it also connects ingredients that might otherwise feel like a hodgepodge. When you consider that vinaigrettes and marinades (both mixtures of oil and vinegar or a stand-in like citrus juice) aren't so different after all, other dressings can also operate as double agents. Try marinating with currant-anchovy vinaigrette (page 18) for even more salty-and-sweet back-and-forth, preserved lemon vinaigrette (page 32) on summer squash or fish, and definitely romesco (page 43).

If you can't find fresh figs, skip the fruit grilling. Halve the plumpest dried ones you can find, macerate them in a few tablespoons of the marinade (look: *triple* duty!) until softened, and then toss them into the salad with a good drizzle of vinaigrette, of course.

1. To make the vinaigrette, whisk together the vinaigrette ingredients until emulsified. Taste and adjust the seasoning. Wipe the mushrooms clean with a damp paper towel. Using a small spoon, scrape out and discard the gills.

2. Arrange the mushrooms in a wide, shallow dish and brush all over with half of the vinaigrette. Let marinate at room temperature for at least 30 minutes, or up to a few hours, turning the mushrooms a few times.

3. Meanwhile, coat half of the figs with vinaigrette. Thread them onto skewers (you can also grill them directly on the grill grates).

4. Heat the grill to medium-high and brush your grates clean. Grill the mushrooms, reserving the marinade, until tender when pierced with a knife, 4 to 5 minutes per side. Grill the figs until lightly browned, about 2 minutes per side.

5. Cut the mushrooms into thin strips. Season the arugula with a few pinches of salt, then toss with the remaining vinaigrette, a little at a time, until evenly and lightly coated. Add the Pecorino, almonds, mushrooms, and grilled and fresh figs and toss together. Drizzle with a little more vinaigrette before serving.

Roasted Potato Salad with Mustard-Walnut Vinaigrette

Roasted roots + garlicky, mustardy vinaigrette + nuts + herbs + egg topper

Serves 6 to 8 | From Shannon Hulley

4 pounds (1.8kg) mixed marble potatoes or other small potatoes

Extra-virgin olive oil, for drizzling

Sea salt and freshly ground black pepper

1 bunch scallions, white and green parts, thinly sliced

6 to 8 eggs

1 cup (100g) walnuts, toasted and coarsely chopped

Leaves from 1 bunch basil, torn

Mustard-Walnut Vinaigrette

2 garlic cloves

Sea salt

2 tablespoons freshly squeezed lemon juice

1 tablespoon red wine vinegar

1 tablespoon whole-grain mustard

1 tablespoon Dijon mustard

¼ cup (60ml) extra-virgin olive oil

2 tablespoons walnut oil

Freshly ground black pepper

This potato salad celebrates its namesake ingredient, the humble and excellent spud, instead of allowing it to drown in a bowlful of gloppy white dressing. Roasted until browned, the potatoes themselves are the stars, and after a light mash, get to bathe in a mustardy vinaigrette. Basil adds a surprising freshness, toasted walnuts play up the potatoes' roasted side, and all of the flavors together will speak to you even at room temperature. So without the soft-boiled egg on top, this salad is good for potlucks, picnics, and backyard parties. Celebrate accordingly.

1. Heat the oven to 425°F (220°C). Arrange the potatoes in a single layer on two parchment-lined, rimmed baking sheets, drizzle with olive oil, and toss to evenly coat. Season with salt and pepper. Roast, shaking the sheets occasionally, until tender and brown, 40 to 45 minutes.

2. To make the vinaigrette, place the garlic on a cutting board, sprinkle with a couple of generous pinches of salt, and finely chop and smash it into a paste with the side of a chef's knife. Whisk together the garlic paste, lemon juice, vinegar, and both mustards until smooth. Gradually whisk in the olive and walnut oils until emulsified. Taste and adjust the salt and pepper.

3. Transfer the potatoes to a large bowl. Toss in the scallions and the vinaigrette. Using the back of a mixing spoon, gently smash some of the potatoes just enough to break the skins. Be careful not to make mashed potatoes. Allow the dressed potatoes to sit at room temperature for 45 to 60 minutes.

4. About 15 minutes before serving, bring a pot of water to a boil (or to steam the eggs, see page 62). Lower the eggs, a few at a time, into the water and boil for 6 minutes. Remove the eggs with a slotted spoon, plunge them into an ice bath until cool enough to handle, and then peel them (page 62).

5. Just before serving, stir in the walnuts and basil. Arrange the salad on plates. Top each serving with a soft-boiled egg and sprinkle with salt and pepper.

Roasted Broccoli Rabe, Chickpea & Crispy Salami Salad

Roasted things of all sorts (vegetables, beans, bread, meat) + romesco

Serves 4 | From Emily Connor

1 pound (450g) broccoli rabe, trimmed

Kosher salt

3 cups (500g) cooked chickpeas

3 ounces (85g) salami, cut into ½-inch (1.3cm) cubes

8 ounces (225g) day-old sourdough or ciabatta bread, crusts removed, cut into ¾-inch (2cm) cubes

Romesco Vinaigrette

¼ cup (25g) sliced almonds, toasted

1 roasted red bell pepper, jarred or freshly roasted

2 tablespoons sherry vinegar, plus more as needed

1 tablespoon tomato paste

1 garlic clove

1 teaspoon Spanish smoked paprika

6 tablespoons (90ml) extra-virgin olive oil

3 tablespoons water, plus more as needed

½ teaspoon sugar, plus more as needed

Kosher salt

Amanda Hesser dubbed romesco a "sauce hero" that gets along with just about everything in the kitchen. So of course this rugged almond, tomato, and red bell pepper sauce can slip into the role of vinaigrette with ease. Before heading into the oven, the salad components get coated with a bit of the dressing—a step we'll use over and over for more fiery roasting. As the salami roasts, it crisps up while its rendering fat slicks the breadcrumbs and chickpeas with, well, salami fat! Whether romesco or salami is the hero of this dish remains unresolved—but know that the real winner is your roasting repertoire.

1. Heat the oven to 500°F (260°C). Line a rimmed baking sheet with parchment paper.

2. To make the vinaigrette, in a food processor, pulse the almonds until finely ground, 20 to 30 seconds. Add the bell pepper, vinegar, tomato paste, garlic, and paprika and process until a paste forms. With the processor running, gradually pour in the olive oil, then the water, and process until emulsified. Add more water to thin the vinaigrette if needed. Add the sugar and season with salt. Taste and adjust seasoning; the vinaigrette should be slightly sweet to balance the bitterness of the broccoli rabe. (The vinaigrette will keep in an airtight container in the fridge for up to 3 days.)

3. Rinse and dry the broccoli rabe, allowing a bit of water to cling to the leaves. On the prepared baking sheet, evenly coat the broccoli rabe with 3 tablespoons of the vinaigrette and season with salt.

4. Arrange in a single layer and roast until tender and the leaves are lightly charred around the edges, 5 to 8 minutes. Arrange on a cutting board in one layer (stacking will make them soggy). Leave whole, or coarsely chop into bite-size pieces.

5. On a parchment-lined baking sheet (it can be the one you just used), evenly coat the chickpeas and salami with a few tablespoons of the vinaigrette. Spread into a single layer and roast until light brown, about 8 minutes, then stir in the breadcrumbs. Once evenly brown, another 3 minutes, remove from the oven and toss with the rabe. Taste and adjust the seasoning, adding more vinaigrette if desired. Serve warm or at room temperature.

Carrot & Radicchio Salad with Fig-Balsamic Vinaigrette

Roasted roots + bitter greens + toasted nuts + tart-sweet vinaigrette

Serves 4 | From Kenzi Wilbur

2 pounds (900g) multicolored carrots, scrubbed and halved lengthwise

½ cup (120ml) extra-virgin olive oil

Kosher salt

¼ cup (60ml) water

1 medium to large head radicchio

½ cup (60g) pistachios, toasted and coarsely chopped

Fig-Balsamic Vinaigrette

½ cup (90g) diced fresh figs or 2 large dried figs, stemmed

¼ cup (60ml) balsamic vinegar

2 tablespoons water

Kosher salt

½ cup (120ml) extra-virgin olive oil

1 small shallot, minced

You won't need to push aside filler ingredients to get to more consequential components in this salad, inspired by a dish from Max and Eli Sussman's book *Classic Recipes for Modern People*. It starts with sweet carrots that are steam-roasted in the oven with a bit of water (this is the secret to incomparably tender carrots). Then it gets piles of raw and roasted ribbons of radicchio, a big boy–size handful of pistachios, and a tart fig dressing that reminds you that you can have a fruity dressing without it being . . . fruity. You could stab recklessly into this thing, blindfolded, and still get a perfect bite. How many other salads would you want to eat with your eyes closed?

1. Heat the oven to 375°F (190°C). In a large bowl, toss the carrots with the olive oil, season with a large pinch of salt, and arrange in a single layer on a rimmed baking sheet. Pour the water over the carrots. Roast until the carrots have just started to brown and crisp on the edges, 20 to 25 minutes.

2. Meanwhile, core and coarsely chop the radicchio and place half of the chopped leaves in a large salad bowl.

3. When the carrots are 5 minutes from being done, scatter the remaining radicchio on top of them so it wilts and begins to brown in spots.

4. To make the vinaigrette, if using fresh figs, in a large bowl, whisk together the figs, vinegar, water, a small pinch of salt, olive oil, and shallot. If using dried figs, blend the figs with the vinegar, water, and a small pinch of salt until smooth. With the blender running, gradually add the olive oil until emulsified. Whisk in the shallot.

5. Add the roasted carrots and radicchio to the salad bowl, drizzle with a bit of vinaigrette (you will not use it all, so start slow), and toss very gently to keep the carrots intact. Add the pistachios and toss again. Taste, adjust the seasoning, and add more dressing if the salad looks dry. Serve warm or at room temp.

Charred Broccoli & Lentil Salad

Charred vegetables + lentils + shredded roots + tahini dressing + nuts/herbs/cheese
Serves 4 | From Emily Connor

2 cups (400g) green
lentils, rinsed and
picked over

1 yellow onion, peeled
and halved

2 bay leaves

2 heads broccoli

Kosher salt

Olive oil, for coating

1 cup (110g) grated carrots
(from 2 or 3 carrots)

1 large handful fresh flat-
leaf parsley, leaves and
stems coarsely chopped

2 ounces (55g) feta,
cut into small cubes

⅓ cup (40g) pistachios,
coarsely chopped

**Smoky Tahini
Dressing**

1 jarred or freshly
roasted piquillo or red
bell pepper, seeded

1 garlic clove

3 tablespoons tahini,
stirred in the jar

3 tablespoons water,
plus more as needed

2 tablespoons extra-
virgin olive oil

1 tablespoon sherry
vinegar, plus more
as needed

1 teaspoon honey

1 teaspoon Spanish
smoked paprika

¼ teaspoon red pepper
flakes, plus more as
needed

¼ teaspoon kosher salt,
plus more as needed

Humble its parts may be, but trust us, this is salad as friend: What starts out as slaw-like—a pile of shredded carrots and broccoli heads and stalks put through a mandoline—quickly gains heft. Lentils are folded into smoky-sweet tahini dressing while still steaming hot. That broccoli? Passed under the broiler until dark in spots and pliant, a ribbon of green that folds and curls throughout. Then in go tiny cubes of feta, showers of parsley and pistachios. Add a splash of sherry vinegar if it's calling for a little pluck.

1. Place lentils, onion, and bay leaves in a saucepan and cover by at least 1 inch (2.5cm) of water. Bring to a boil, then turn down the heat and simmer until the lentils are tender, about 30 minutes. Keep a watchful eye, adding additional water if needed. Drain well in a colander, discarding the onion and bay leaves.

2. Remove the leaves from the broccoli and cut any discolored areas off the stems. Cut the heads lengthwise into quarters. Using a mandoline, the slicing blade of a food processor, or a sharp knife, cut the broccoli stems and florets into ¼-inch (6mm) slices.

3. Heat the broiler with an oven rack 4 to 5 inches (10 to 13cm) from the flame. Place the broccoli (including the little florets that break off while slicing) on a baking sheet, season with salt, and evenly coat with olive oil. Spread in a single layer, leaving plenty of room in between the slices (you may need 2 sheets). Broil the broccoli until tender and charred, 3 to 5 minutes, shaking the pan once or twice.

4. To make the dressing, blend all of the ingredients until smooth. Add more water to thin the dressing if needed. Taste and adjust the seasoning. (The dressing will keep in an airtight container in the refrigerator for up to 3 days.)

5. In a large bowl, evenly coat the lentils and carrots with the tahini dressing, a little at a time. Add more vinegar, red pepper flakes, and salt to taste. Fold in the broccoli, followed by the parsley and feta. Fold in the pistachios just before serving. Serve warm or at room temperature. (The salad will keep in an airtight container in the refrigerator for up to 3 days; it's good right from the fridge.)

Shaved Brussels Sprouts, Endive & Apple Salad

Raw and sautéed vegetables + croutons + more crunchies + rich, warm dressing

Serves 4 | From Emily Connor

1 pound (450g) brussels sprouts, trimmed and thinly sliced with the slicing blade of a food processor, mandoline, or sharp knife

3 endives, leaves stacked and sliced crosswise into ¼-inch (6mm) ribbons

2 ounces (55g) day-old sourdough or ciabatta bread, crust removed, cut into ¾-inch (2cm) cubes

1 small, crisp apple (such as Honeycrisp or Pink Lady), halved, cored, and cut into ⅛-inch (3mm) slices

¼ cup (25g) walnuts, toasted

¼ cup (10g) finely chopped fresh chives

Pancetta-Lime Dressing

3 tablespoons olive oil, plus more as needed

4 ounces (115g) pancetta, finely diced

Grated zest of 1 lime

3 tablespoons lime juice, plus more as needed

1 small chile (such as jalapeño), finely diced

Kosher salt

You've had shaved brussels sprout salad before, but it wasn't as invigorating as it is here. Served warm (though it's also good at room temp), sautéed shredded brussels sprouts meet the richness of pancetta and the snap of breadcrumbs, sliced endive, and apple. In a dish where you'd expect lemon, lime surprises (and keeps those apples from browning, to boot). To lift up leftovers, add a poached egg or chopped chicken or turkey or aged cheddar, or toss in mesclun or arugula. Leftovers can be gently reheated in a skillet or microwave until the sprouts are just warm.

1. To make the dressing, in a 12-inch (30cm) skillet, heat 1 tablespoon of the olive oil over medium heat. Add the pancetta and cook, stirring every so often, until crisp, about 5 minutes. Off the heat, transfer the pancetta to a paper towel–lined plate. Pour the pancetta fat into a small, heatproof bowl, then pour 3 tablespoons of it back into the skillet. (Add olive oil if you need to supplement.) Whisk in the lime zest, lime juice, chile, and a pinch of salt.

2. Return the skillet to medium heat and add the brussels sprouts, tossing well to evenly coat with the dressing. Season with salt and sauté just until the leaves are crisp-tender, 1 to 2 minutes. Transfer the sprouts to a large bowl, add the endive, and toss together.

3. Wipe out the skillet and heat the remaining 2 tablespoons olive oil over medium heat. Add the bread cubes, tossing well to evenly coat, and cook until light brown and crispy, about 3 minutes.

4. Add the bread, crisp pancetta, apple, walnuts, and chives to the brussels sprouts and endive. Toss well. Taste and adjust the seasoning before serving.

When Dressing's "Done"

When it comes time to sample your finished dressing, if you lick it off your finger, you might love the flavor, but not once it's on the salad. That's because dressings are meant to complement a salad, so taste it the same way: Dip a main component of your salad into the dressing instead of your finger and you won't have any surprises with the end result.

Grain & Bean Salads

Toasted Farro & Asparagus Salad

Crispy grains + sautéed vegetable "pebbles" + nuts + crumbly cheese + herbs + citrus

Serves 4 | From Emily Connor

2 pounds (900g) thin asparagus

6 tablespoons (90ml) extra-virgin olive oil, plus more as needed

1½ cups (270g) pearled farro

Kosher salt

1 tablespoon unsalted butter

½ teaspoon red pepper flakes, or to taste

Grated zest of 1 lemon

3 tablespoons freshly squeezed lemon juice, or to taste

½ cup (60g) pistachios, finely chopped

3 ounces (85g) French feta, cut into ¼-inch (6mm) cubes

⅓ cup (15g) coarsely chopped fresh tarragon

Sometimes you want to use your fork to poke around a salad, excavating the wily arugula leaves and camouflaged croutons. Other times—tonight, maybe—you don't want dinner to be an archaeological dig; you want a salad with more consistency, though just as much excitement. To make crispy bits of asparagus you won't have to hunt down, take a tip from Thomas Keller: Cut the stalks crosswise into thin coins, then crisp them up with the longer, stubbly tops and the farro. A fork—or better, a spoon—will cradle them with farro and tiny cubes of feta, each bite as focused with lemon, red pepper, and tarragon as the next.

1. Snap off the tough bottoms of each asparagus spear; discard or save them for asparagus soup or another use. Gather the spears into a bundle, cut off the tips and cut the spears into ¼-inch (6mm) coins.

2. In a wide saucepan or Dutch oven, heat 2 tablespoons of the olive oil over medium-high heat. Add the farro and stir to coat the grains evenly. Cook, stirring occasionally, until toasted, 3 to 5 minutes. Add a generous pinch of salt and enough water to cover the farro by at least 2 inches (5cm). Bring to a boil, then turn down the heat and simmer until the farro is al dente, about 25 minutes. Drain.

3. While the farro is cooking, in a large skillet, heat 1 tablespoon of the olive oil, the butter, and red pepper flakes over medium-high heat, stirring a few times so the pepper flakes evenly toast, just a couple minutes. Working in batches if needed, add the asparagus tips and sauté for about a minute, then add the asparagus coins and continue cooking, stirring occasionally, until the tips and coins are bright green and crisp-tender, a minute or two more.

4. Add the drained farro to the asparagus. Add the lemon zest and juice and 2 tablespoons extra-virgin olive oil, tossing well to combine. Taste and adjust the seasoning. Add up to another tablespoon of olive oil, if you like. Let cool for about 10 minutes, then add the pistachios, feta, and tarragon and toss again. Serve warm or at room temperature. (The salad will keep in an airtight container in the refrigerator for a day; bring to room temperature before serving.)

Grilled Ratatouille & Bulgur Salad

Fluffy grain + grilled vegetables + nuts/herbs/cheese

Serves 4 | From Emily Connor

2 tablespoons olive oil, plus more for coating

1 cup (140g) bulgur

2 cups (475ml) vegetable or chicken stock

Kosher salt and freshly ground black pepper

1 or 2 Asian eggplants, trimmed and halved lengthwise

2 zucchini or yellow squash, trimmed and halved lengthwise

1 large tomato, cored and halved

1 large sweet onion cut crosswise into ½-inch (1.3cm) rounds

1 large red bell pepper, halved and seeded

3 ounces (85g) feta, cut into chunks

⅓ cup (30g) sliced almonds, toasted

1 cup (20g) loosely packed basil leaves, torn

¼ cup (5g) loosely packed mint leaves, torn

Lemon-Tahini Dressing

¼ cup (60ml) extra-virgin olive oil

Grated zest of 1 lemon

2 tablespoons freshly squeezed lemon juice

2 teaspoons tahini, stirred in the jar

¼ teaspoon sumac or piment d'Espelette (optional)

¼ teaspoon kosher salt, plus more as needed

In this salad, the elements of CSA-gobbling ratatouille don't slouch into a stew, but rather get charred and diced up, bounced around with bulgur and a flurry of herbs and toasty almonds and cheese, then misted with lemony tahini dressing. Emily Connor calls this salad "ratatouille that's taken a detour to the Middle East." That's true, though it's also dinner tonight and lunch, cold, tomorrow.

1. In a 2-quart (1.9L) saucepan, heat the olive oil over medium heat. Add the bulgur and cook, stirring occasionally, until the bulgur is golden and fragrant, 4 to 5 minutes. Add the stock and bring to a boil. Cover, turn down the heat, and simmer until the bulgur is tender and the stock is absorbed, 15 to 20 minutes. Drain well and spread evenly on a rimmed baking sheet to cool and prevent clumping.

2. To make the dressing, whisk all of the dressing ingredients together until emulsified. Taste and adjust the seasoning. Drizzle half of the dressing over the bulgur, tossing to evenly coat. Season with salt.

3. Heat the grill to medium and brush your grates clean, or heat a grill pan over medium-high heat. Evenly coat the eggplants, zucchini, tomato, onion, and bell pepper with olive oil. Season with salt and pepper. When the grill is hot, grill the vegetables, turning occasionally, until moderately charred and tender. This could take a few minutes for the tomato and up to 10 minutes for the bell pepper and onion. Transfer the grilled vegetables to a cutting board, let cool, then coarsely chop into bite-size pieces.

4. Spread the bulgur out on a large serving platter. Top with the cooled grilled vegetables and toss with a little more dressing until the salad is well coated. Scatter over the feta, almonds, basil, and mint. Serve warm or at room temperature.

The Hot List

While slightly smoky Aleppo pepper is different from the not-crazy-hot piment d'Espelette or robust chile de árbol, most dried chiles are fairly interchangeable, so pick the chile you like best and use it whenever red pepper flakes are called for. Which chiles make up generic red pepper flakes, anyway?

Smoked Lentil Salad with Sriracha Miso Mayo

Smoked lentils + spicy mayo + raw, crisp veg

Serves 4 | From Nancy Brush

8 ounces (225g) green lentils, rinsed and picked over (preferably Le Puy)

1 teaspoon ground cumin

1 teaspoon garlic powder

1 teaspoon onion powder

¼ cup (60ml) olive oil

1 tablespoon minced garlic

1 cup (160g) roughly diced yellow onion

3 celery stalks, cut into large dice

Kosher salt

3 carrots, sliced into coins

1½ cups (355ml) low-sodium vegetable stock

½ cup (45g) mesquite or hickory chips

1 cup (105g) diced cucumber

1 cup (180g) diced fresh tomatoes

½ cup (80g) diced sweet onions (such as Vidalia or Walla Walla)

Freshly ground black pepper

Sriracha Miso Mayo

½ cup (120ml) mayonnaise

¼ cup (70g) white miso paste

1 teaspoon sriracha

The first thing that struck us about this salad was how it smelled. The next was that the smoky scent was wafting not from bacon or a fire pit but from *lentils.*And then we were smitten. While lentils can be smoked outside on your grill, this is the opportunity to make your house smell like a campfire without setting off a temperamental fire alarm—hacking a smoker with a Dutch oven, colander, and mesquite or hickory chips. The smoking process is totally fun and mesmerizing—the cooked lentils turn red and take on a heartiness they've never known.

While you might assume the rich smokiness is overwhelming or one-note, the sriracha miso mayo adds acid, salt, and earthiness. The fresh vegetables are important—they provide texture—but feel free to play with whatever you've got. Serve this salad as shown on page ix on a slightly burnt piece of toast (char begets char), or over a pile of greens, or alongside a burger to get ample use from your grill.

1. In a large, heatproof bowl, combine the lentils, cumin, garlic powder, and onion powder and cover with boiling water. Soak, covered, for 20 minutes, then drain well and set aside.

2. In a large Dutch oven, heat the olive oil over medium-high heat. When the oil begins to shimmer, turn the heat to medium, add the garlic, and sauté for 30 seconds. Add the onion and celery and season with salt. Cover and cook, stirring occasionally, until the onion is translucent, 3 to 5 minutes. Stir in the carrots, drained lentils, and stock, turn the heat to high, and bring to a boil. Immediately turn down the heat and simmer, covered, until the lentils are just tender, 15 to 20 minutes. Spread the lentils evenly on two rimmed baking sheets to let cool and prevent clumping.

3. Meanwhile, cover the wood chips with water in a small bowl and let soak for 20 minutes. Drain.

4. If you're smoking the lentils on the stove, line the bottom of a large Dutch oven with heavy-duty aluminum foil, add the soaked wood chips, cover the pot, and turn the heat to high. Pour one baking sheet of lentils into a colander. Once the wood chips start smoking, set the colander in the pot, and re-cover the pot (you could add a layer of foil if the lid isn't fitting well). Smoke for

10 minutes. Turn off the heat, keeping the pot closed, and let the smoke subside for 5 minutes. The lentils will turn a little red. If you're smoking the lentils on the grill, wrap the soaked wood chips in heavy-duty aluminum foil and pierce the foil several times. Heat the grill to medium-high. Place the wood chips near the grill's heating element (or according to your grill's directions), and close the grill. After 10 minutes, place one baking sheet of lentils on the grill grates, close the grill, and smoke for 10 minutes. Turn off the heat, keeping the grill closed, and let the smoke subside for 5 minutes. Leave the second baking sheet of lentils unsmoked.

5. To make the mayo, stir together the mayonnaise, miso, and sriracha until combined. Cover and refrigerate until ready to use.

6. Let the lentils cool to room temperature. Transfer the smoked and unsmoked lentils to a large bowl and gently fold half of the mayonnaise in. Cover and refrigerate until chilled, 2 to 4 hours.

7. Stir in the cucumber, tomato, and onion. Fold in the remaining mayo, sprinkle with pepper, and serve.

Genius Tip: Pickled Grains

These wunderkinder of make-ahead lunches can be toasted (page 53) but also pickled— a trick we found in the pages of *Everyday Whole Grains* by Ann Taylor Pittman. Imagine a grain in caper form, and you have a pickled grain. To make a cup (175g), in a pot, combine 1½ cups (355ml) apple cider vinegar or white wine vinegar, 3 tablespoons sugar, 1 teaspoon kosher salt, a bay leaf, a dried red chile, and whatever whole spices you like to pickle with. Bring to a boil and cook until the sugar dissolves, about 3 minutes. Stir in a cup (160g) of cooked hard grains (farro, millet, wheat berries, spelt, or kamut—soft grains like barley will mush). Remove from the heat, let cool to room temperature, then transfer to an airtight container and refrigerate for 1 hour before sprinkling on salads. Store in the fridge for up to 2 weeks.

Coconut Rice Salad with Mango, Bell Pepper & Lime

Grain + lentils + fruit + warming spices + herbs

Serves 4 | From Emily Connor

Kosher salt

1 cup (185g) basmati rice, rinsed

½ cup (95g) brown lentils, rinsed and picked over

¼ cup (60ml) vegetable oil or ghee

1 teaspoon cumin seeds

½ teaspoon black mustard seeds

2 teaspoons peeled, grated fresh ginger

⅔ cup (50g) unsweetened dried coconut flakes

⅓ cup (50g) salted roasted peanuts

Grated zest of 1 lime

2 to 3 tablespoons freshly squeezed lime juice

1 large or 2 small mangoes, cut into matchsticks

1 large bell pepper, seeded and cut into matchsticks

1 cup (20g) loosely packed fresh cilantro leaves

1 Fresno or jalapeño chile, cut into thin rings

This salad proves that with a little primp and polish, your favorite side can easily become your main squeeze. Studded with fried lentils, fresh chiles, and salty nuts, coconut rice is a popular Indian dish that often costars alongside curries or dals, but adding mango, crunchy bell pepper, and the zing of lime juice brings it center stage. Because the ingredients hold up, this salad is equally delicious warm or at room temperature—several hours or even a day after making it. Serve it with a dollop of yogurt and more cilantro than you think you need.

1. Bring two large pots of salted water to a boil. Stir the rice into one pot and the lentils into the other. Return the pots to a boil, then turn down the heat and simmer until tender but not mushy, 10 to 12 minutes for the rice and 15 to 20 minutes for the lentils. Drain the cooked rice and spread it evenly on a rimmed baking sheet to cool and prevent clumping. Drain the lentils in a colander and let cool.

2. In a large skillet, heat the vegetable oil over medium-high heat. Add ¼ cup (50g) of the cooked lentils, the cumin seeds, and the mustard seeds and fry until the lentils start to crisp, 2 to 3 minutes. Add the ginger and cook for a minute or so until fragrant. Then add the coconut flakes and peanuts, stirring well, and continue to fry until the coconut turns light golden, another minute or two. Remove from the heat and stir in the lime zest. Measure out ¼ cup (35g) for garnish.

3. In a large serving bowl, combine the rice, lentils, and remaining fried lentil-coconut mixture. Add the lime juice and a pinch of salt. Fold in the mango, bell pepper, cilantro, and chile. Sprinkle the reserved fried lentil-coconut mixture over the top and serve warm.

Farro & Golden Beet Salad with Chive-Sage Dressing

Hardy grains + roasted roots + candied nuts + crumbly cheese + herby dressing

Serves 4 | From Emily Nichols Grossi

3 golden beets, trimmed

Extra-virgin olive oil, for sprinkling

Kosher salt and freshly ground black pepper

1¾ cups (415ml) vegetable stock

1 cup (180g) pearled farro

⅓ cup (40g) pecans

2 tablespoons maple syrup

Small pinch of cayenne pepper

⅓ cup (50g) good-quality crumbled feta

Chive-Sage Dressing

⅓ cup (80ml) extra-virgin olive oil

1 tablespoon plus 1 teaspoon chopped fresh chives

1 teaspoon chopped fresh sage

Juice of ½ lemon

1 teaspoon kosher salt

¼ teaspoon freshly ground black pepper

There is something so beautiful—and reassuring—about a dish you can make at the beginning of the week in under an hour and pack for lunch every day, knowing it's only going to get better as the week goes on. This is one of those salads: It's hearty enough to keep you full until dinner, with enough going on flavor- and texture-wise (earthy-sweet beets, creamy feta, sautéed-herb dressing, just-spicy candied pecans!) that it keeps you interested—very interested. For even more intrigue, add a spice-fried egg (page 62).

1. Heat the oven to 400°F (200°C). Place the beets in the center of a big piece of foil on a baking sheet. Coat with some olive oil and salt and pepper. Fold the foil to make a packet and crimp the edges. Bake the beets until tender (you can check by piercing a fork through the foil), 45 to 60 minutes, depending on their size. Remove from the oven. When cool enough to handle, remove them from the foil and peel off the skin. Coarsely chop.

2. Meanwhile, pour the stock into a 2-quart (1.9L) saucepan, cover, and bring to a boil. Pour in the farro, then turn down the heat and simmer until the farro is just on the tender side of al dente, 15 to 25 minutes. Drain well.

3. To make the dressing, in a small saucepan, heat the olive oil over medium-high heat until very warm. Off the heat, whisk in the chives, sage, lemon juice, salt, and pepper. Let rest in the pan so the flavors meld.

4. Coat a piece of aluminum foil with nonstick cooking spray. Put the pecans in a small skillet and set over medium heat. When the skillet is warm, add the maple syrup and cayenne. Stir continuously until the pecans are evenly coated and the syrup bubbles nicely, about 5 minutes. Pour the pecan mixture onto the prepared foil, let cool, and then coarsely chop.

5. In a bowl, toss together the farro, beets, pecans, and feta. Whisk the dressing again and pour it over the salad. Stir gently until well combined. Season with salt, then eat.

Easy Eggs

Genius Tip: Spice-Fried Eggs

Frying an egg in hot olive oil, basting it as lovingly as you do a Thanksgiving turkey, results in an egg with crispy edges and a runny center. You probably already know that. But adding spices to that warm oil is a teensy upgrade that you can execute even at your hangriest. As the spices simmer in the oil, they toast and round out, turning plain ol' cooking oil into a luscious sauce. Canal House's version adds ½ teaspoon of smoked paprika to 4 tablespoons of olive oil before cracking 4 eggs in the pan. The eggs get seasoned with salt, then basted with the oil with a spoon—turning down the heat if it gets too hot. The eggs are then served with the oil spooned over—electric with spice and color. But we couldn't stop there, frying our eggs in turmeric, cumin, harissa, za'atar, chile flakes, cayenne (and not worrying too much about the measurements—it's fried eggs, not physics).

Egg Salad Every Which Way

Once they're cool, chop the eggs according to your mood—the shape doesn't affect the flavor. Feeling type A? Use an egg slicer to make straight-sided pieces. Too tired to deal with sharp tools? A butter knife will break the eggs into jagged edges. We won't tell anyone if you just tear up the eggs with your hands. Whether you're more of a mayonnaise or Greek yogurt type, choose a neutral binding agent with at least a little fat to bring the egg salad together. Olive oil would do the trick; Merrill uses cottage cheese! Your accompaniments can be as simple as a squiggle of yellow mustard and a tablespoon or two of apple cider vinegar. But you could also add celery for crunch, dill and chives for additional oomph, and diced capers and cornichons for a briny bite. The key is to use a similar size dice for all of the ingredients (including the eggs). Anything you'd add to an omelet (bacon, fresh or sun-dried tomatoes, feta) would be welcome here. Taste as you go, adjusting the seasoning with salt and pepper as you like.

How to Poach Eggs

Bring a wide saucepan with 3 to 4 inches (7.5 to 10cm) of water to a boil. Crack an egg into a ramekin, then gently shift it into a fine-mesh sieve, letting some of the white drain from the yolk. Shimmy the egg back into the ramekin, then slip it into the boiling water. Let the egg simmer until the white is opaque, a few minutes. Use a fine-mesh sieve or slotted spoon to remove your perfectly poached, wisp-less egg, then repeat as necessary.

Don't Boil Eggs—Steam Them!

Every person has their way of hard-boiling eggs—"Start with cold water!" "No, the water has to be boiling!"—but a steamer crushes the competition (and really, starting with cold water makes the eggs harder to peel, so start with boiling if you don't steam). When you steam eggs, the whites become tender and the yolks are anything but chalky. The eggs are evenly cooked, in little time (because you're boiling only a bit of water instead of a potful).

To hard- or soft-cook your eggs in a steamer: Bring 1 inch (2.5cm) of water to a boil in a big pot with a metal steamer inside. Transfer your eggs directly from the fridge to the steamer—we can fit 6 without overcrowding. Cover the pot and let the eggs cook for 12 minutes for hard-boiled and 6 minutes for soft-boiled. Transfer the eggs to an ice bath, let them chill out until you can handle them, then peel or refrigerate until you're ready for them.

How to Peel Boiled Eggs

The keys to quickly and easily peelable eggs are water and cold eggs. In an ideal world, you'd refrigerate the cooked eggs overnight before peeling. But in the real world if you have just minutes, submerge the eggs in a bowl of cold water until they're cool enough to handle. Then, use the bowl's rim to crack the egg and gently peel underwater. The water acts as gentle wedge as you pry the shell from the egg white. The shells float to the top, leaving you with just your peeled eggs.

Radish & Pecan Grain Salad

Grains of all sorts + protein + herbs + crunch + dried fruit + vinegar

Serves 4 | From Amanda Hesser

2 cups (360g) mixed grains (such as pearled farro, freekeh, wheat berries, wild rice, quinoa, pearl barley, or any combination)

1 cup (125g) cubed roast turkey

1 cup (115g) radishes (ideally watermelon or French breakfast), thinly sliced with a mandoline

1 cup (20g) loosely packed baby arugula leaves

1 cup (20g) loosely packed fresh flat-leaf parsley leaves, minced

1/2 cup (10g) loosely packed fresh tarragon leaves, minced

1/2 cup (10g) loosely packed fresh mint leaves, cut in a chiffonade

1/2 cup (50g) pecans

1/2 cup (75g) raisins

1/2 cup (60g) dried cranberries

1/4 cup (60ml) walnut oil

1/4 cup (60ml) sherry vinegar

1/4 cup (40g) minced shallots

1/4 cup (60ml) olive oil

1/4 teaspoon kosher salt, plus more as needed

As Amanda put it, "This is the kind of salad that sounds like a starchy do-gooder, but it has grace and conviction." Adapted from Court Street Grocers in Brooklyn (and shown on page ii, facing the title page), it'll teach you that you can cook all different grains together in the same pot, so long as you time it right. It'll show you that different oils (here, walnut) will pay off in their ability to backbone in a way olive oil just can't, and it won't slap you on the wrist if your fridge isn't bursting with the season's best. Here's where to put your dried cranberries, raisins, pecans, and other pantry lurkers.

1. Bring a large pot of generously salted water to a boil. Add the grains, turn down the heat, and simmer until just tender, about 25 minutes. (With grains like wild rice and wheat berries, add them to the pot first and cook 10 minutes before adding the remaining grains).

2. Drain the grains in a colander, then set aside until warm to the touch.

3. In a large bowl, combine all of the ingredients and toss well. Adjust seasonings to taste and serve warm or at room temperature.

Genius Tip: Bulk-Toasting Nuts, Just Do It

For a small amount of nuts, we're the first to stick them in a skillet over low heat till they smell like themselves. But for toasting in bulk, the oven is the way to go—especially if you heat it to a lower temperature than you might think. Our creative director, Kristen Miglore, picked up this tip when she was a whippersnapper-intern at *Saveur* magazine's test kitchen. The director at the time, Hunter Lewis, who's now the editor at *Cooking Light*, likes to toast nuts on a rimmed baking sheet at 325°F (165°C). Because the oils are gently coaxed out, the nuts are more evenly toasted and less prone to burning in the blink of an eye. Nuts will take anywhere from 5 minutes (pistachios) to 15 (whole almonds and hazelnuts)—though use these times just as a guideline. Your nose should decide when the nuts are toasty.

Instead of toasting precisely the amount of nuts a recipe calls for, toast a whole bag at once so they're always at the ready. They will keep in an airtight container at room temperature for up to a month or in the freezer up to a year.

Sprouted Mung Bean, Carrot & Date Salad

Sprouts, grains, or beans + crunchy veg and nuts + dried fruit + tart vinaigrette + yogurt

Serves 4 | From Emily Connor

8 Medjool dates, pitted and quartered lengthwise

2 tablespoons freshly squeezed lemon juice

1 cup (105g) sprouted mung beans (page 66)

4 carrots, thinly sliced into rounds

2 celery stalks, thinly sliced crosswise

½ cup (50g) walnuts, toasted and coarsely chopped

¼ cup (5g) loosely packed cilantro leaves

1 avocado, peeled, pitted, and chopped

Kosher salt

Pomegranate Vinaigrette

2 tablespoons minced shallots

1 tablespoon pomegranate molasses

Grated zest of 1 lemon

2 tablespoons freshly squeezed lemon juice, plus more as needed

¼ cup (60ml) olive oil

Kosher salt and freshly ground black pepper

Dill-Yogurt Sauce

¾ cup (175ml) Greek yogurt

1 tablespoon olive oil

1 tablespoon finely chopped fresh dill

½ teaspoon kosher salt

The mung bean, fixture of the 1970s, gets new life in sprout form: They're like nature's Pop Rocks, surprising at every bite. We really urge you (in a no-pressure, nonviolent sort of way) to sprout the beans yourself (page 66). They're the brightest thing to come out of your pantry, so much cheaper than store-bought versions, and really simple to make—plus, it's thrilling to *finally* grow something on the windowsill. (If you're feeling antsy, cooked beans or grains, such as spelt or wheat berries, can sub in.) The salad gets chic with its lemon-macerated dates, sultry pomegranate molasses vinaigrette, and an herby yogurt sauce—but still a little crunchy with the sprouts and carrots, celery and walnuts too.

1. In a small bowl, toss together the dates and lemon juice. Let macerate.

2. To make the vinaigrette, in a bowl or jar, whisk together the shallots, pomegranate molasses, lemon zest and juice, and olive oil. Season with salt, pepper, and add more lemon juice to taste. In a separate bowl, stir the yogurt sauce ingredients.

3. Put the dates and any remaining lemon juice into a large bowl. Add the mung beans, carrots, celery, walnuts, cilantro, and avocado. Add the vinaigrette, a tablespoon at a time, and gently toss with your hands until the ingredients are evenly dressed. Season with salt and more lemon juice.

4. Spoon a puddle of the sauce on each plate and top with the salad. This salad can be made several hours in advance and served at room temp (though add the avocado right at the end).

Pomegranate Molasses DIY

Once you realize that making pomegranate molasses is essentially boiling pomegranate juice for an hour and change, why continue your endless hunt for the store-bought stuff? To make this tart, ruby-red syrup yourself, cook 4 cups (950ml) pomegranate juice, ½ cup (100g) sugar, and 2 tablespoons freshly squeezed lemon juice over medium heat, stirring occasionally, until the sugar dissolves. Turn down the heat to medium-low and cook until the mixture gets thick and syrupy and reduces to 1 cup (240ml), 70 to 80 minutes. Let cool for 30 minutes before transferring to a glass jar, where it can live in your fridge for up to 6 months.

How to Sprout Your Own Grains, Beans & Seeds (No Sunshine Required)

In a matter of days, give the grains, beans, and seeds languishing in your pantry a fresh start—and give yourself a seriously nutritious, delicious ingredient to play with. All you need is a jar with a lid, a bowl, some cheesecloth, a rubber band or twine, and a few days.

What can sprout?

You can sprout just about any whole grain, bean, or seed that's raw and hasn't been treated in any way, such as spelt, rye, kamut, buckwheat, barley, oats, einkorn, rice, wheat berries, millet, chickpeas, soybeans, mung beans, quinoa—or the seeds of alfalfa, broccoli, chia, radish, kale, sesame, sunflower, or mustard. Most can be found at your grocery store or a natural foods store. Some nuts that are truly raw and not pasteurized—like peanuts and almonds—can also sprout, though shelled nuts like walnuts or pistachios cannot.

How long does sprouting take?

It depends on what you're sprouting and the temperature in your house, but smaller ingredients, like quinoa, sprout just a day after soaking and heartier seeds, like alfalfa, can take up to 5 days. You only need to pay attention to this affair for about 5 minutes in the morning and at night, and if you forget to rinse once or twice, they'll still sprout just fine.

How do I do it?

1. In a jar with a lid, combine 1 part whole grain, seed, or bean to 3 parts filtered water. To make enough sprouts for a few salads and sandwiches, start with about ½ cup (about 90g) of grain or beans or a few tablespoons of seeds (they expand a lot). Cover the top of the jar with two layers of cheesecloth secured with twine or a rubber band, and let soak out of direct sunlight at room temperature for 8 to 12 hours.

2. Turn the jar upside down into the sink and drain the water through the cheesecloth. Shake the jar a few times to make sure all of the liquid is drained.

3. Remove the cheesecloth, refill the jar with water, screw on the lid, and shake to rinse. Then, remove the lid, re-cover the jar with cheesecloth secured with twine, and drain into the sink, shaking to get out all the water so mold doesn't grow.

4. Place the jar in a bowl at an angle, with the cheesecloth pointing down so the beans continue to drain. Let sit at room temperature, out of direct sunlight, for 8 to 12 hours.

5. When you check at this point, you may have sprouts. If you don't, repeat steps 3 and 4 until you do. The sprouts are ready when they have tails roughly the same length as their bodies. The sprouts will keep in an airtight container in the refrigerator for 3 to 5 days.

Salads That Like Sprouts

Wild Rice Bowl with Tofu, Sweet Potatoes & Roasted Shallot Vinaigrette

Grain + tofu + roasted roots and alliums + hearty greens

Serves 4 | From Emily Connor

1 (14-ounce/396g) package extra-firm tofu

1 cup (240ml) balsamic vinegar

1 tablespoon Dijon mustard

½ teaspoon honey

Olive oil, for roasting

Kosher salt

1 pound (450g) sweet potatoes, peeled and cut into ¾-inch (2cm) cubes

¾ cup (120g) wild rice or wild rice blend

1 small bunch lacinato kale, stemmed, deribbed, and cut into thin ribbons

1 small tart apple, chopped into cubes

3 ounces (85g) aged cheddar, crumbled or cut into cubes

Roasting marinated tofu is one of the most hands-off ways to prepare it, and you end up with firm, glazed cubes with a concentrated flavor. Plus, your oven is a multitasker in a way your sauté pan can't be. While the tofu bakes, you'll also roast cubes of sweet potatoes and thin slices of shallots—same temperature, same time. The sweet potatoes get tossed into the kale along with wild rice, apple, and crumbled cheddar, but the softer, tamer shallots are whisked into a vinaigrette (you can use the same technique with scallions, onions, or leeks). If you're crunched for time, skip the marinade altogether and simply brush the tofu with olive oil and season with salt and pepper before roasting. The vinaigrette, made with many of the same ingredients that are in the marinade, can carry the salad.

1. Wrap the tofu snugly in 4 or 5 layers of paper towels and place on a plate. Cover with a second plate and place a heavy can on top to press the tofu; set aside to let drain for at least 30 minutes (this is great to do the morning you plan to cook the tofu). Discard the paper towels. Cut the tofu into ¾-inch (2cm) cubes.

2. Stir together the vinegar, mustard, and honey. Add the tofu and marinate for 30 minutes to 1 hour. Drain and discard the marinade.

3. Meanwhile, place the shallot for the vinaigrette in the center of a piece of aluminum foil, toss with a few teaspoons of olive oil and a pinch of salt. Fold the foil to make a packet.

4. Position oven racks in the top third and lower third of the oven. Heat the oven to 400°F (200°C). Line two baking sheets with parchment paper.

5. Arrange the marinated tofu in a single layer on one of the baking sheets and brush with olive oil. On the second sheet, toss the sweet potatoes with enough olive oil and salt to evenly coat. Arrange the sweet potatoes in a single layer and place the shallot packet alongside. Roast the tofu and sweet potatoes, rotating the baking sheets halfway through, until the tofu is golden brown and just crisp and the sweet potatoes are golden brown and tender, 35 to 40 minutes.

CONTINUED

**Roasted Shallot
Vinaigrette**

1 large shallot, trimmed
and thinly sliced
lengthwise

2 tablespoons balsamic
vinegar

2 teaspoons freshly
squeezed lemon juice,
or to taste

¼ teaspoon honey,
or to taste

¼ cup (60ml) extra-
virgin olive oil

Kosher salt and freshly
ground black pepper

6. Meanwhile, cook the wild rice according to package directions. Every blend has a slightly different cooking time, but a general rule of thumb is to combine 1 part rice to 4 parts water, simmer covered, and start checking at the 45-minute mark. The rice should be chewy, and some of the grains may have burst open. Drain and let cool.

7. To make the vinaigrette, using a stand or immersion blender, blend the roasted shallot, vinegar, lemon juice, honey, extra-virgin olive oil, ¼ teaspoon salt, and ¼ teaspoon pepper until emulsified. Taste and adjust the seasoning, adding more lemon juice if needed.

8. In a large bowl, combine the tofu, sweet potatoes, wild rice, kale, apple, and cheddar. Toss in the vinaigrette, a little at a time, until the salad is evenly dressed. Taste and adjust the seasoning. Serve warm or at room temperature.

The Last Drops of Dijon

There hasn't been a utensil created—yet—to get at that mustard that clings to the side of its jar. So work with the stubborn stuff (jam, too!): Add a bunch of dressing ingredients to the jar (oil, vinegar or lemon, salt, and pepper). Close the jar, give it a shake, and not only will it bend to your wishes, but you have a dressing that's already in its portable container.

Dressing's Second Act

A dressing is really just a sauce, isn't it? So, for vinegar- or citrus-based vinaigrettes, use them in place of oil, salt, and pepper when cooking vegetables, beans, and proteins. Drizzle over grilled fish, chicken, or sausage; use it as the start of a pasta sauce; or marinate meat and seafood in it. Creamy dressings can be used as a dip for crudités or wherever else mayo makes an appearance—as a sandwich spread or in chicken, egg, or tuna salads.

Mushroom & Mixed Grains Salad with Carrot-Harissa Vinaigrette

Grains + roasted mushrooms and greens + earthy vinaigrette + cheese

Serves 4 | From Emily Connor

1 pound (450g) cremini, button, or shiitake mushrooms (or a mixture), stemmed and cut into bite-size pieces

¼ cup (60ml) olive oil

1 tablespoon finely chopped fresh thyme

Kosher salt

1 large bunch Swiss chard, stemmed, deribbed, and torn into bite-size pieces

2 cups (about 380g) mixed grains (such as farro, spelt, sorghum, and pearled barley)

4 ounces (115g) ricotta salata, crumbled

½ cup (45g) sliced almonds, toasted

Carrot-Harissa Vinaigrette

½ cup (120ml) carrot juice

2 tablespoons sherry vinegar

1 tablespoon freshly squeezed lemon juice, plus more as needed

2 teaspoons harissa, or to taste

1 garlic clove, minced

¼ teaspoon honey, or to taste

½ cup (120ml) extra-virgin olive oil

Kosher salt

Tossed, still-warm, and with an electric-orange vinaigrette, this is not your granny's grain salad. There are welcome nubs of roasted mushrooms, handfuls of wilted Swiss chard, and pebbles of ricotta salata to bring it back from the brink of virtuousness. Make it with whatever grains you love—now's also your chance to try the spelt and sorghum you've been curious about at the natural foods store. Just do not skip the dressing! Built on sweet, snappy carrot juice and spice (go ahead, add more harissa if you like), it takes a bowl of classically "earthy" ingredients and casts them in sunlight.

1. Heat the oven to 375°F (190°C). Toss together the mushrooms, 2 tablespoons of the olive oil, and the thyme on a parchment-lined rimmed baking sheet. Season with salt and spread into a single layer. Roast the mushrooms for 20 minutes, then spoon off any liquid that's accumulated so the mushrooms can brown. Roast until brown and tender, 5 to 10 minutes more, then transfer the mushrooms to a large plate to cool.

2. Toss together the chard and remaining 2 tablespoons olive oil on the same parchment-lined baking sheet. Season with salt, then really get in there with your hands and massage the oil into the chard until evenly coated. Roast until the leaves start to wilt, 3 to 5 minutes. Let cool on the baking sheet.

3. To make the vinaigrette, whisk or blend all of the ingredients until emulsified. Taste and adjust the seasoning, adding more harissa or lemon juice if needed. (The vinaigrette will keep in a glass jar in the refrigerator for up to 3 days.)

4. Cook each grain separately, or cook them together in a large pot with enough water to cover by at least 6 inches (15cm), adding grains at intervals depending on their cooking times. When the grains are cooked, drain well and transfer to a large bowl or serving dish. Let cool a few minutes, then toss with about half of the vinaigrette. Toss with the mushrooms, chard, ricotta salata, and almonds. Taste and adjust the seasoning, then drizzle in more vinaigrette and toss again until evenly dressed. Serve warm or at room temperature. (The salad will keep in an airtight container in the refrigerator for up to 3 days.)

Freekeh, Fennel & Smoked Fish Salad

Grain + pungent veg + smoked protein + herbs + crumbly cheese + citrus

Serves 4 | From Barbara Reiss

1 cup (230g) cracked or whole freekeh, cooked according to package directions and drained

½ cup (75g) crumbled feta

½ cup (70g) finely chopped Kalamata olives

1 cup (125g) flaked hot-smoked trout, or to taste

½ cup (20g) finely chopped fresh flat-leaf parsley

½ cup (25g) finely chopped fresh mint

1 small fennel bulb with fronds, minced

2 scallions, white and light green parts, minced

Grated zest of 1 orange

Orange Dressing

⅓ cup (80ml) fruity olive oil

¼ cup (60ml) freshly squeezed orange juice

2 tablespoons rice vinegar

Kosher salt and freshly ground black pepper

It's the itty-bitty bits that make this salad powerful: wisps of orange zest, a scattering of Kalamata olives, feta crumbles, and herb confetti throughout. There's also the deep smokiness of the hot-smoked trout that wakes up every bite. You can find the firm, flaky, very smoked fish next to lox at the market. Fennel haters, be forewarned: By mincing up a whole bulb, you get all the fiery complexity without any aggressive bitterness, so don't skip it. This is the salad that will make you a believer. A sturdy base of freekeh means it will keep on the go and for a few days in the fridge, but you could swap in any hardy cooked grain.

1. In a serving bowl, toss together the freekeh, feta, olives, trout, parsley, mint, fennel, scallions, and orange zest.

2. To make the dressing, whisk together the dressing ingredients until emulsified. Season with salt and pepper.

3. Add dressing to the salad, a little at a time, and toss just until coated. Taste and season with salt and pepper before serving.

Genius Tip: Crunchy Crumbled Tempeh

Tempeh—tofu's heartier, crumblier cousin—can be hard to love, but we think this is its best effort. In *How to Cook Everything Vegetarian*, Mark Bittman explains that his tempeh cracklings can be used "how you might use grated cheese, only it doesn't melt." The fried tempeh reminds us of a crunchy grain, like farro, with a little protein thrown in. To make it, heat 2 tablespoons neutral oil in a large skillet over medium-high heat. With two forks or your fingers, crumble as much tempeh as you want into the hot oil. Cook, stirring frequently, until the tempeh is deep brown and crispy, 5 to 7 minutes. Stir in your favorite spices, chopped herbs, or chile paste, if you like. With a slotted spoon, transfer the tempeh to a paper towel–lined plate to drain. Season with kosher salt and freshly ground black pepper and eat immediately—on top of a salad, tacos, eggs, roasted vegetables, or toasts—or let cool, cover tightly, and refrigerate for up to 3 days.

Brown Butter Brussels Sprouts
& Crispy Quinoa

Toasty quinoa + roasted vegetables + macerated fruit + nuts/herbs/cheese

Serves 4 | From Emily Connor

1/2 cup (65g) dried apricots, julienned

2 tablespoons sherry vinegar

1 tablespoon plus 1 teaspoon freshly squeezed orange juice

1/4 cup (60g) unsalted butter

4 anchovy fillets, minced

1 teaspoon grated orange zest

1/4 teaspoon red pepper flakes, or to taste

1 1/2 pounds (680g) brussels sprouts, trimmed and halved lengthwise or quartered if they're large

Kosher salt

1 1/2 cups (280g) cooked quinoa

2 tablespoons olive oil

3/4 cup (15g) loosely packed fresh flat-leaf parsley leaves

1/4 cup (30g) roasted hazelnuts, coarsely chopped

1 (2-ounce/55g) chunk aged Manchego, cubed

Quinoa can so often be more fluff than substance, a bit of nothingness stuck in your teeth. But here's a cooking method that yields crispy-chewy quinoa: Broil until they snap, crackle, pop. This toasted quinoa isn't just better in texture, it's also better at clinging to vegetables—here, they're a crispy crust on brussels sprouts that are roasted in a brown butter–anchovy sauce. Which, yes, is also good on carrots, summer or winter squash, potatoes, tomatoes, you name it. Oh, did we mention the sherry vinegar–macerated apricots? We—for once—got too excited about the quinoa.

1. Heat the oven to 425°F (220°C). Toss together the apricots, vinegar, and 1 tablespoon orange juice and let macerate.

2. In a small pan, melt the butter over medium heat and cook until it turns brown and smells nutty, about 5 minutes. Stir frequently, scraping up any browned bits from the bottom so they don't burn. Off the heat, immediately stir in the anchovies until they dissolve. Stir in the orange zest, red pepper flakes, and remaining teaspoon of orange juice.

3. Place the brussels sprouts on a parchment-lined baking sheet, pour the brown butter–anchovy mixture over the top, and toss until evenly coated. Season with salt and spread into a single layer. Roast, stirring occasionally, until tender and golden brown with a few singed leaves, 15 to 20 minutes. Remove from the oven.

4. Pour a couple tablespoons of the apricots' liquid over the brussels sprouts and season with salt. Toss and let cool a bit.

5. Heat the broiler with an oven rack 4 to 5 inches (10 to 13cm) from the flame. With the cooked quinoa spread on a baking sheet, toss with the olive oil, then spread into a thin, even layer. Broil until you hear a faint popping sound, a few minutes. Stir, spread out, and repeat until the quinoa is lightly brown and crispy, 5 to 7 minutes total.

6. In a large serving bowl, toss together the brussels sprouts, apricots and their liquid, parsley, hazelnuts, Manchego, and half of the quinoa. Scatter the remaining quinoa over the top. Serve warm or at room temperature.

Roasted Chickpea Salad with Za'atar

Warmed beans and veg + fried alliums + herbs + citrus + sweetness

Serves 4 | From Shruti Jain

1 (15-ounce/425g) can chickpeas, drained and rinsed

3½ teaspoons extra-virgin olive oil

Grated zest and juice of 1 lemon

2 teaspoons za'atar

Kosher salt

¼ teaspoon freshly ground black pepper

2 garlic cloves, minced

1 small carrot, thinly sliced

½ fennel bulb, thinly sliced

¼ head red cabbage, thinly sliced

¼ cup (5g) loosely packed fresh mint leaves, coarsely chopped

1 tablespoon raisins

1 tablespoon maple syrup

1 shallot, thinly sliced and fried (see below)

Crumbled feta, for garnish (optional)

Eaten straight from the pan or over a bowl of something comforting (like polenta or savory oats), this salad makes a sunny meal in a season of browns and beiges, stews and meat. Za'atar, mint, lemon, raisins, and maple syrup make the flavors just as exciting as the color scheme, and the textures are surprising too: thinly sliced vegetables sautéed until they're relaxed and chickpeas that are roasted at a low temperature so they crisp on the outside but stay soft when you bite in. For crunchy-all-the-way-through chickpeas, bake at a higher heat (425°F/220°C) for 30 to 35 minutes, stirring frequently, until browned. This salad becomes more of a slaw if you leave the cabbage, fennel, and carrot raw. For a creamy variation, add dill and yogurt to the dressing.

1. Heat the oven to 250°F (120°C). On a parchment-lined baking sheet, stir together the chickpeas and 1½ teaspoons of the olive oil. Stir in the lemon zest and some of the lemon juice, the za'atar, 1 teaspoon salt, and pepper, then spread into a single layer. Bake until toasted, 10 to 15 minutes.

2. In a large sauté pan, heat the remaining 2 teaspoons of olive oil over high heat. Add the garlic and cook until fragrant, 30 seconds. Add the carrot, fennel, and cabbage and cook until just wilted, about 5 minutes.

3. Remove the pan from the heat and stir in the roasted chickpeas, mint, raisins, and maple syrup. Taste and add more lemon or salt if needed. Transfer to a serving plate and top with the fried shallot and feta. Serve warm, at room temperature, or cold.

How to Make Perfectly Crispy Fried Shallots—Without Flour

Skip the flour-dredging and pay attention to your pan's heat and you—and your salads, soups, stews, and snacking—can get not burnt, not oil-soaked, perfectly crisp shallots. Here's how our test kitchen chef, Josh Cohen, does it. Slice the shallots so that they're super thin (preferably with a mandoline), then place them in a pan of room-temperature—yes, room-temperature—canola or another neutral oil. Turn up the heat to high and watch the shallots bubble. Then turn the heat to medium. When the bubbles subside, it means that the moisture has cooked off the shallots (they should look golden brown). Transfer to a paper towel–lined plate to let cool. Sneak a spoonful, then scatter liberally.

White Bean Salad with Fennel Three Ways

Creamy beans + broiled veg and citrus + crunch + olives

Serves 4 | From Emily Connor

2 fennel bulbs with fronds

2 lemons

3 tablespoons extra-virgin olive oil

Kosher salt and freshly ground black pepper

3 cups (540g) cooked white beans (such as cannellini, Great Northern, or an heirloom variety)

½ cup (70g) pitted Castelvetrano olives, halved

¼ teaspoon red pepper flakes, or to taste

To make salads better, a normal impulse is to add more ingredients, but instead of crowding your grocery cart, coax everything you want from one vegetable. It'll be a superhero, and you: scrappy. Here, fennel is shaved and broiled with whole lemon slices and diced raw for crunch, while its fronds stand in for herbs. Once mixed with beans (canned if you want to eat in 15 minutes) and lemon dressing, you'll have a salad that'll keep for days. Fennel, you look good with a red cape on.

1. Remove the fennel fronds, coarsely chop, and set aside. Remove the tough, outer layer of the fennel bulbs, then halve each bulb lengthwise and core. Using a mandoline or sharp knife, thinly slice one and a half fennel bulbs lengthwise. Finely dice the remaining half bulb.

2. Cut one of the lemons into half-moons. Discard the seeds. Juice the remaining lemon and set aside.

3. Heat the broiler with an oven rack 4 to 5 inches (10 to 13cm) from the flame. Toss togeher the sliced fennel, sliced lemon, and 1 tablespoon of the olive oil on a parchment-lined baking sheet. Season with salt and spread the fennel and lemon slices in a single layer. Broil, shaking the baking sheet once or twice, until the fennel is tender and lightly charred in spots, 3 to 5 minutes.

4. Toss the cooked beans with the broiled fennel and lemon, the raw fennel, the remaining 2 tablespoons of olive oil, the olives, 2 tablespoons lemon juice (or to taste), red pepper flakes, and fennel fronds. Season with salt and pepper. (The salad will keep in an airtight container in the refrigerator for up to 3 days.) Serve warm, cold, or at room temperature.

How to Soak Your Beans, Stat

If you wanted to soak your dried beans, like, yesterday, all hope isn't lost. Put the beans in a pot and cover them with 1 inch (2.5cm) of water. Cover and bring to a boil, then turn off the heat and let the beans soak for an hour. Drain and continue as if you'd planned to quick-soak your beans all along.

Pasta & Bread Salads

Baby Artichoke, Fregola & Pistachio Aillade Salad

Small starch + crispy vegetables + garlic + sharp cheese/other flavor bombs

Serves 4 | From Emily Connor

3 to 3½ pounds (1.4 to 1.6kg) baby artichokes (15 to 18)

Juice of 1 small lemon

3 tablespoons olive oil

Kosher salt

¼ teaspoon red pepper flakes, or to taste

⅔ cup (160ml) white wine, such as Sauvignon Blanc

2 tablespoons capers

1 cup (185g) fregola

2 tablespoons freshly squeezed lemon juice, or more to taste

2 ounces (55g) Pecorino Romano, crumbled or finely chopped

¼ cup (5g) loosely packed fresh mint leaves, coarsely chopped or torn

1 cup (20g) loosely packed fresh flat-leaf parsley leaves (fried, if desired, see page 10)

Pistachio Aillade

½ cup (60g) unsalted shelled pistachios

2 garlic cloves, coarsely chopped

Kosher salt

Grated zest of 1 lemon

½ cup (120ml) extra-virgin olive oil

We've long been fans of chef April Bloomfield's pot-roasting technique for baby artichokes, wherein their cut sides get golden-brown and their bodies softened by white wine. But why stop there? Heaps of beadlike pasta soak up the caper-flecked, wine-drunk sauce, and then you top the whole thing with pistachio aillade—a coarse mash-up of pistachios, garlic, and lemon zest. Given baby artichokes' short window, know that this salad is a worthwhile occasion—special even if you use brussels sprouts in their place or don't fry your parsley.

1. To make the aillade, cook the pistachios over medium heat just long enough to warm through, 2 to 3 minutes. With a mortar and pestle (or sharp knife or mini food processor), pound the garlic with ½ teaspoon of salt until a paste forms. Add the pistachios and pound into small, irregularly shaped pieces. Stir in the lemon zest and olive oil. Taste and adjust the seasoning.

2. Remove the outer leaves of the artichokes until you get to the pale yellow-green tender center. With a paring knife or sharp vegetable peeler, cut off the stem and trim the fibrous part around the base. Cut the top inch (2.5cm) off. Fill a large bowl with cold water and add the lemon juice and artichokes.

3. In a large heavy pot or sauté pan with a lid that's wide enough to hold the artichokes in a single layer, heat the olive oil over medium-high heat. Add the artichokes, cut side down, season with salt and the red pepper flakes, and cook, undisturbed, for 3 minutes. Pour in the wine, cover the pan, and turn down the heat. Simmer, without stirring, until you can insert a knife into the artichoke bottoms without any resistance, 10 to 12 minutes. Remove the lid, add the capers, turn the heat to medium-high, and bring the wine to a boil. Cook until the wine evaporates and the cut sides are golden brown, 3 to 5 minutes. Turn down the heat, if needed, to prevent scorching. If not much wine has evaporated at this point, you can pour all but a few tablespoons off so the artichokes brown.

4. Meanwhile, bring a large pot of generously salted water to a boil. Add the fregola and cook until al dente, or according to the package directions. Drain.

5. In a large bowl, stir together the fregola, half of the aillade, and the lemon juice. Season with salt. Add the artichokes, capers, Pecorino, mint, and parsley. Drizzle more aillade over and serve warm or at room temperature.

Spring Vegetable Panzanella

Toasted bread + herby sauce + vegetables of all sorts + cheese + egg topper

Serves 4 to 6 | From Sarah Jampel

¼ cup (60ml) extra-virgin olive oil

1 baguette or small loaf ciabatta, cut into 1-inch (2.5cm) cubes (3 or 4 cups)

Kosher salt and freshly ground black pepper

1 leek, white and light green parts, cleaned and cut into very thin circles

1 bunch asparagus, trimmed and cut into 2-inch (5cm) pieces

2½ cups (350g) English peas, fresh or frozen

2 large handfuls snow peas, trimmed

2 teaspoons balsamic vinegar, or to taste

Juice of ½ lemon

6 ounces (170g) Parmesan, finely chopped or crumbled

4 to 6 eggs (optional, for on top)

Pesto Dressing

1½ cups (30g) loosely packed fresh basil leaves

½ cup (25g) loosely packed fresh mint leaves

4 thyme sprigs

2 tablespoons walnuts

1 or 2 garlic cloves

¼ cup (60ml) extra-virgin olive oil

¼ cup (25g) finely grated Parmesan

Kosher salt (optional)

Panzanella doesn't have to be exclusively a platform for tomatoes; when you're stuck in spring, and impatient, it can be about the greens that peep up just in time to save you from winter's stupor. To replace the moisture that typically comes from the tomatoes, here's a garlicky three-herb pesto. It cozies the hunks of bread, crumbles of Parm, and crew of vegetables that have relaxed into buttery sautéed leeks. (Full disclosure: This salad is nearly half bread.)

1. In a large skillet, heat 3 tablespoons of the olive oil over medium-low heat. Add the bread cubes and 1 teaspoon salt and stir until the cubes are evenly coated. Cook, stirring occasionally, until golden brown, about 10 minutes. Transfer to a serving bowl and wipe out the pan.

2. To make the pesto, in the bowl of a food processor, process the basil, mint, leaves from the thyme sprigs, walnuts, garlic, and 2 tablespoons of the olive oil until a paste forms. With the processor running, gradually pour in the remaining 2 tablespoons of olive oil and process until the paste is thinner, smoother, and paler. Add the grated Parmesan and pulse until just incorporated. Taste and adjust the seasoning; if you're worried about the pesto browning, transfer it to an airtight container.

3. In the same skillet, heat the remaining tablespoon of olive oil over medium-low heat. Add the leek and a fat pinch of salt and cook, stirring frequently, until the leek has started to break down, 5 to 7 minutes. Be careful not to cook the leek too quickly—you want it to slowly disintegrate.

4. Add the asparagus and sauté, stirring frequently, until bright green, 3 to 4 minutes. Add the English peas and snow peas and cook, still stirring, until similarly vivid, 2 to 3 minutes more (you don't have to cook the snow peas if they're lively raw). Taste to make sure they're still peppy but not raw.

5. Dump the vegetables onto the bread. Add half of the pesto, the vinegar, lemon juice, and Parmesan; season with pepper; and toss together until everything is shiny with pesto. Add more pesto if necessary. Let the panzanella mingle while you poach the eggs (page 62).

6. Scoop the panzanella into bowls and gingerly position a poached egg atop each bowl if you like. Serve immediately.

Bagna Cauda Egg Salad on Rye Toast

Toast + egg + garlicky anchovy dressing + leaves + crunchy veg

Serves 4 | From Emily Connor

12 hard-cooked eggs (page 62), quartered or sliced

2 celery stalks, thinly sliced on the diagonal

¾ cup (35g) celery leaves or mix of celery leaves and fresh flat-leaf parsley leaves

5 large radishes, thinly sliced

Sea salt and freshly ground black pepper

8 thick slices rye bread, toasted

4 leaves Bibb lettuce

Bagna Cauda Dressing

10 olive oil–packed anchovy fillets

3 garlic cloves, coarsely chopped

½ cup (120ml) extra-virgin olive oil

2 tablespoons unsalted butter

¼ teaspoon red pepper flakes

Grated zest and juice of 1 lemon, plus more lemon juice if needed

Kosher salt

This stunner from Emily Connor will not just feed you well, it will teach you many things: to cook garlic and anchovies *before* adding them to your vinaigrette; to toss everything while the dressing is still warm so the vegetables, in her words, "slacken" just enough; to never throw away celery leaves again. Emily knows you'll think about skipping the celery, but don't. It adds a needed spring and vitality. And the toast? It's there, but for us it's all about the salad.

1. To make the dressing, mash the anchovies and garlic into a smooth paste using a mortar and pestle, sharp knife, or mini food processor. Transfer the paste to a small saucepan, add the olive oil, butter, and red pepper flakes, and bring to a bare simmer over low heat; you should faintly hear the garlic and anchovy sizzle, and the anchovy and butter should melt into the oil. Cook for about 5 minutes, then remove from the heat. Whisk in the lemon zest and juice until emulsified, then season with salt. Taste and adjust the seasoning, adding more lemon juice if needed.

2. In a large bowl, combine the eggs, celery, celery leaves, and radishes. Add the dressing, a little at a time, and gently toss to coat. You want an assertively dressed but not overdressed salad. Season with salt and pepper, then taste and adjust the seasoning, adding more lemon juice if needed. (The egg salad will keep in an airtight container in the refrigerator for up to 2 days; let sit at room temperature for 20 minutes before serving.)

3. Brush each slice of toasted rye with the dressing, top with a big leaf of lettuce, season with salt and pepper, and pile high with egg salad. Eat immediately with a fork and knife, or just pick it up and prepare to be messy.

Treat Lettuce Like the Veg It Is

If you want a vegetable to taste good, you must season it. You already know this, but do you salt and pepper your lettuces before dressing them? It's a dead-simple step that brings out the flavor of the greens, regardless of how many embellishments you add to the bowl.

Lemony Greek Pasta Salad

Warm pasta or grain + briny things + crunch + soft cheese + herby, lemony dressing
Serves 4 | From Sarah Fioritto

Kosher salt

1 pound (450g) orzo pasta

2 cucumbers, halved
lengthwise, seeded,
and sliced

1 cup (135g) Kalamata
olives, pitted and sliced

6 ounces (170g) feta,
crumbled

**Lemon-Dill
Vinaigrette**

Grated zest of 1 lemon

2 tablespoons freshly
squeezed lemon juice

2 teaspoons Dijon
mustard

1 shallot, grated

Kosher salt and freshly
ground black pepper

5 tablespoons (75ml)
extra-virgin olive oil

¼ cup (10g) fresh dill
leaves, chopped

This salad doesn't get boring because it's a spot-on version of a salad you probably already know and love (ahem, Greek salad). The ingredients are thoughtfully layered so they all make their mark. Just take a look at the vinaigrette: Grated shallot and mustard embolden it, and the dill gets stirred into the dressing instead of scattered over as garnish. Then, when the dressing coats the still-warm pasta, all the bold flavor sticks to each orzo kernel. There aren't any tomatoes potentially watering down the salad, either; only cucumbers for crunch and briny olives and feta. Make a big batch and it'll keep on giving: Add new things to it as days go by—a handful of chickpeas, grilled eggplant, canned tuna. Serve it alongside grilled chicken, salmon, or lamb. And if it's ever feeling bland, just hit it with lemon juice and the flavors will spring right back.

1. Bring a large pot of generously salted water to a boil. Add the orzo and cook according to the package directions. Drain and transfer to a large salad bowl.

2. Meanwhile, make the vinaigrette: Whisk together the lemon zest and juice, mustard, and shallot. Add a few pinches of salt and pepper. Gradually whisk in the olive oil until emulsified, then stir in the dill. Taste and adjust the seasoning as needed.

3. Pour the vinaigrette over the still-warm pasta and toss to evenly coat. Let cool to room temperature, about 25 minutes, then fold in the cucumbers and olives. Scatter the feta over the top and serve. Leftovers will keep in the fridge for up to 4 days. Bring to room temp before eating.

How to Pit Olives Without a Fancy Contraption

From the department of "dull but necessary kitchen tasks," as Amanda calls them, is our recommendation for the best way to pit an olive. After senior staff writer Sarah Jampel performed an extensive test of all reasonable ways to pit an olive—including with a frying pan, potato masher, even a paper clip—she deemed our founders' methods the best across all types of olives. Amanda goes at her olives with a meat pounder: Smash, smash, smash until you feel the pit. Merrill uses a similar technique, but she bangs with the flat side of her kitchen knife to separate the olive from the pit.

Grilled Bread, Broccoli Rabe & Summer Squash Salad

Grilled bread + creamy marinade + grilled vegetables + toasted nuts + herbs

Serves 4 | From Emily Connor

1 large bunch broccoli rabe or young broccoli

3 summer squash, cut into ½-inch (1.3cm) rounds

¼ cup (60ml) extra-virgin olive oil, plus more as needed

4 thick slices crusty bread (such as ciabatta or sourdough)

Kosher salt and freshly ground black pepper

¼ cup (35g) toasted pine nuts or chopped almonds

Handful of torn fresh basil and mint

Freshly squeezed lemon juice, for drizzling

Mayonnaise Marinade

1 cup (240ml) full-fat mayonnaise

½ cup (120ml) olive oil

Grated zest and juice of 2 lemons

2 garlic cloves, mashed into a paste

1 tablespoon kosher salt

1 tablespoon cumin seeds

1 teaspoon Aleppo pepper or ½ teaspoon red pepper flakes

1 teaspoon Spanish smoked paprika

A warning if your glass is half empty, an instruction if it's half full: Marinate your vegetables in mayonnaise once and never look back. On the grill, the creamy sauce turns into a blistery crust, shielding broccoli rabe and summer squash from incineration while permeating the vegetables with chile-heat. Win, win, win. Once you've got the papery rabe leaves and the charred squash rings, all you need is a whole lot of glorified croutons (that's the "grilled bread"), some fun accessories (pine nuts, basil, and mint—a lo-fi pesto), and the freedom to eat the whole thing with your hands, licking your fingers between bites.

1. To make the marinade, in a large bowl, whisk together the mayonnaise, olive oil, lemon zest and juice, garlic, salt, cumin seeds, Aleppo pepper, and paprika until smooth and emulsified.

2. Trim the broccoli rabe stalks. Cut any stalks that are more than ½ inch (1.3cm) thick lengthwise. Rinse to remove any grit, allowing a bit of excess water to cling to the leaves, which will help steam the stalks on the grill.

3. Add the broccoli rabe and summer squash to the marinade and toss to coat. Let marinate at room temperature for about 30 minutes, tossing occasionally.

4. Meanwhile, heat the grill to medium. Brush your grates clean, then brush with olive oil. Working in batches if necessary, arrange the broccoli rabe and squash in a single layer on the grill. They're done when tender and nicely blistered in spots, a few minutes per side. If the stalks are charring quickly but still aren't tender, drizzle a few drops of water on them. Transfer the vegetables to a baking sheet and spread in a single layer (stacking will cause them to lose their crispness).

5. Evenly coat both sides of each bread slice with the olive oil. Season with salt and pepper. Grill the bread, checking it frequently, until charred in spots but soft in the center, a few minutes per side. Turn down the heat if needed. Let cool, then cut into ½-inch (1.3cm) cubes.

6. Place the bread cubes, broccoli rabe, and summer squash on a large serving platter, as artistic or rustic as you like. Scatter the nuts, basil, and mint. Season with salt and pepper, and drizzle with olive oil and lemon juice. Serve warm or at room temperature.

Half-Blistered Tomato Pasta Salad

Starch + roasted and raw tomatoes + soft and hard cheeses + tenders + nuts

Serves 4 | From Emily Connor

1 pound (450g) casarecce or other tubular pasta

2 cups (40g) loosely packed fresh basil leaves, torn if large

¼ cup (5g) loosely packed fresh mint leaves, torn if large

⅓ cup (35g) sliced almonds or ⅓ cup (45g) pine nuts, toasted

4 ounces (115g) fresh mozzarella, torn

1½ ounces (45g) Parmesan, finely chopped or crumbled

Roasted Tomato Vinaigrette

4 cups (540g) cherry tomatoes, halved

4 garlic cloves, peeled

½ cup (120ml) extra-virgin olive oil, plus more for drizzling

Pinch of sugar

Kosher salt

2 tablespoons red wine vinegar or sherry vinegar, or to taste

¼ teaspoon red pepper flakes

When you want a margherita pizza but would rather spend the day at the park than the pizza oven, come right this way. It's all here: roasted *and* raw tomatoes, basil and mint, mozzarella and Parmesan, garlic, but no dealing with dough. Plus, the creamy-not-slick vinaigrette one-ups pizza sauce. It's made from blending oven-burst tomatoes with roasted garlic and red wine vinegar. But you won't miss the pop of fresh cherry tomatoes; those (and more roasted tomatoes) get folded in. After this salad, you'll likely start mixing blistered and raw tomatoes on top of toasted bread or ricotta cheese, in a salsa—doled over pizza, too.

1. To make the vinaigrette, heat the oven to 375°F (190°C). Combine 2 cups (270g) of the cherry tomatoes, the garlic, 2 tablespoons of the olive oil, and the sugar on a parchment-lined, rimmed baking sheet. Season generously with salt, and toss until evenly coated. Spread the tomatoes, cut side up, into a single layer. Roast until the tomatoes have blistered and shriveled, about 1 hour.

2. Blend together the roasted garlic, ¼ cup (50g) of the blistered tomatoes, the vinegar, the remaining 6 tablespoons (90ml) of olive oil, a pinch of salt, and the red pepper flakes. Add more olive oil if needed, a tablespoon at a time, and continue to blend until the vinaigrette is a smooth, creamy consistency. Taste and adjust the seasoning.

3. Meanwhile, bring a large pot of generously salted water to a boil. Cook the pasta until al dente. While the pasta cooks, season the raw tomatoes with salt.

4. Drain the pasta and toss with the vinaigrette in a large bowl. Let the pasta cool until just warm, then toss in the remaining blistered tomatoes, the raw tomatoes and their juices, the basil, mint, nuts, mozzarella, and Parmesan. Taste and adjust the seasoning, then gild the lily by drizzling more olive oil over. Serve at room temperature.

Sort of Tabbouleh with Jammy Onion Vinaigrette

Starch + finely chopped greens + beans + jammy alliums + citrus

Serves 4 | From Ali Slagle

1 teaspoon olive oil

1 cup (170g) Israeli couscous

1½ cups (355ml) water

Kosher salt and freshly ground black pepper

1 bunch flat-leaf parsley, stemmed (page 10)

2 bunches mint, stemmed (page 10)

4 leaves curly kale, deribbed

2½ cups (415g) cooked chickpeas

¼ to ½ teaspoon allspice

Juice of 1 lemon, plus more to taste

Onion Confit

¼ cup (60ml) olive oil

1½ cups (240g) diced onions (from about 2 onions)

Kosher salt and freshly ground black pepper

¼ cup (35g) pine nuts

¼ cup (40g) dried currants

1 teaspoon red pepper flakes

You won't find this particular tabbouleh in the Middle East, but every side step from tradition is for a reason. Despite what you may have eaten, tabbouleh salad is a green salad with some grain, not the other way around. Here, the greens are coarsely chopped parsley, mint, and curly kale (the curliness provides body that our go-to lacinato just can't). Toasted Israeli couscous stands in for the grain, which is typically cracked bulgur wheat—the pasta adds nuttiness and bulk so the chickpeas don't feel humungous. There's a little allspice, though you could use cinnamon, cloves, coriander, or nutmeg. But where the recipe really goes off-road is with the onions: They laze into a jammy confit with pine nuts and currants, a trifecta Merrill perfected in her onion confit recipe. Whereas tabbouleh's onions usually jolt and prick, here they're seductive, softening the roughest edges of an already rugged salad.

1. To make the confit, in a Dutch oven or sauté pan, heat the olive oil over medium heat. Add the onions and a pinch of salt and pepper, then cook, stirring occasionally, until the onions start to soften, about 5 minutes. Turn the heat the lowest it can go and stir in the pine nuts, currants, and red pepper flakes. Simmer, stirring occasionally, until the mixture turns jammy, about 25 minutes. Let cool.

2. While the confit is simmering, heat the olive oil in a saucepan over medium heat. Add the couscous and toast, stirring occasionally, until it turns a light brown color, a minute or two. Add the water and a big pinch of salt, turn the heat to medium-low, cover, and cook until the couscous is tender and the water is absorbed, 7 to 10 minutes.

3. Stir the confit into the couscous, oil and all. Let cool, then refrigerate while you chop the greens.

4. Meanwhile, finely chop the parsley, mint, and kale. You'll get the cleanest cuts if you do forceful, purposeful chops instead of sporadic mincing. Transfer to a big bowl and season with salt and pepper.

5. Add the couscous to the herbs, making sure to get all the confit oil. Stir in the chickpeas, allspice, and lemon juice, and season with salt and pepper. Taste and adjust the seasoning, adding more allspice and lemon juice if needed.

Peanut Noodle Salad

Peanut sauce + noodles + herbs + protein + crunch

Serves 4 | From Sara Jenkins

6 ounces (170g) soba noodles (preferably green tea soba)

1 tablespoon sesame oil

3 tablespoons grapeseed or other neutral oil

1 pound (450g) firm tofu

Kosher salt and freshly ground black pepper

¼ cup (5g) loosely packed fresh basil leaves (preferably small Thai basil leaves)

¼ cup (5g) loosely packed fresh cilantro leaves

¼ cup (30g) bean sprouts

Phuong's Peanut Sauce

½ cup (120ml) water, plus more as needed

6 tablespoons (95g) creamy natural peanut butter, stirred in the jar

¼ cup (60ml) red wine vinegar

2 tablespoons soy sauce

1½ tablespoons peeled, grated fresh ginger

1 tablespoon Asian chile paste

1 tablespoon sesame oil

1 tablespoon dry sherry

1 tablespoon minced garlic

1 teaspoon sugar

½ teaspoon kosher salt

New York City–based chef and Food52's chef in residence Sara Jenkins doesn't consider herself proficient in Asian cooking, but when she gets time away from her Italian restaurant kitchens, it's the cooking she turns to. Her peanut noodles are by no means traditional: The base is Japanese soba—green tea soba if she can find it, though she uses spaghetti in a pinch—and the dressing, which she learned from an old roommate, gets its acidity from red wine vinegar and dry sherry and its spice from any Asian chile paste. The blend-and-you're-done sauce is not so gloppy that it coats your tongue, nor so sweet that you wonder where the jelly is. The other elements are really cook's choice, but if tofu is what's sounding good, Sara's method is about to become your go-to. Rather than fight individual pieces in burbling hot oil, Sara sears the whole block, one side at a time, *before* she cuts it. Each cube will get crunchy tops and bottoms, without the flipping frenzy.

1. To make the sauce, blend all of the ingredients until smooth.

2. Bring a large pot of water to a boil. Add the soba noodles and blanch for 5 to 8 minutes, or according to the package directions. Drain the noodles, rinse in cold water, and transfer to a big bowl. Toss with the sesame oil to coat. Toss with the peanut sauce.

3. In a sauté pan, heat the grapeseed oil over medium-high heat. Place the tofu in the pan, season with salt and pepper, and fry until golden on one side, just a few minutes. Flip and fry until the second side is crisp and golden. Transfer to a paper towel–lined plate, let cool a bit, then cut into bite-size pieces.

4. Top the peanut noodles with the fried tofu, basil, cilantro, and bean sprouts. Serve immediately.

Curried Cauliflower Fattoush

Fried bread + sturdy veg + flavor punches + spiced yogurt dressing

Serves 4 | From Emily Connor

1 large head cauliflower, trimmed and cut into small florets

2 Persian cucumbers or ½ English cucumber

5 radishes, thinly sliced

1 poblano chile

¾ cup (15g) loosely packed fresh cilantro leaves

½ cup (70g) pitted Castelvetrano olives

1 (15-ounce/425g) can chickpeas, drained and rinsed

⅓ cup (50g) raisins

1 tablespoon freshly squeezed lemon juice, or to taste

Kosher salt

2 tablespoons olive oil

3 small pitas, torn into bite-size pieces

Curry-Yogurt Dressing

½ cup (120ml) Greek or plain yogurt

6 tablespoons (90ml) extra-virgin olive oil

Grated zest of 1 lemon

2 tablespoons freshly squeezed lemon juice

1 tablespoon white wine vinegar

1 garlic clove, minced

Kosher salt

2 teaspoons curry powder, or to taste

One of the best parts of trying a new dish is borrowing from it for your own cooking routine. This fattoush has roots in high places—San Francisco's Bar Tartine as well as chefs Thomas Keller and Yotam Ottolenghi—but in the home kitchen, it settles into an ideal make-ahead meal that gets better with age. As time goes by, a zippy curry-yogurt dressing shrugs the crunch off raw cauliflower, and the chickpeas commingle with a punchy crew of poblano chile, olives, cucumbers, raisins, and radishes. Just be sure to throw in the fried pita right before serving.

1. To make the dressing, in a large bowl, whisk together the yogurt, olive oil, lemon zest and juice, vinegar, garlic, ¼ teaspoon salt, and curry powder until smooth. Taste and adjust the seasoning. Because curry powders can vary so much, you might want to add up to a teaspoon more.

2. Add the cauliflower and toss to coat. Marinate for at least an hour, or up to a day. Meanwhile, cut the cucumbers into ½-inch (1.3cm) dice, thinly slice the radishes, stem and cut the poblano into ⅛-inch (3mm) slices, and coarsely chop the cilantro and olives.

3. Add the chickpeas, cucumbers, radishes, poblano, cilantro, olives, and raisins to the marinated cauliflower, tossing to combine. Add the lemon juice, season with salt, and toss again. (The salad will keep in an airtight container in the fridge for up to 1 day; bring to room temperature before serving.)

4. In a large skillet, heat the olive oil over medium-high heat. Working in batches, add the pitas in a single layer, and fry, tossing occasionally, until golden and crispy, 2 to 3 minutes. Transfer to a paper towel–lined plate to dry, then fold the fried pita into the salad. Serve immediately.

Genius Tip: For Less Pucker

For vinaigrettes that start with shallots or garlic, Suzanne Goin of Lucques recommends macerating the alliums in the acid and salt for about 5 minutes before adding the other ingredients. Not only will the alliums relax in pungency, but the salt dissolves and all the flavors get to know each other really well.

Fish & Seafood Salads

Radicchio & Shrimp Salad
with Warm Bacon Vinaigrette

Roasted chicory and protein + warm vinaigrette + herbs + smoke

Serves 2 | From Emily Connor

2 heads chioggia radicchio, trimmed and cut into wedges

3 tablespoons extra-virgin olive oil

1 tablespoon balsamic vinegar

Kosher salt and freshly ground black pepper

1 pound (450g) medium shrimp, peeled, deveined, and tails removed

2 tablespoons finely chopped fresh flat-leaf parsley or chives

Warm Bacon Vinaigrette

1 tablespoon extra-virgin olive oil

3 strips bacon, cut into thin strips

1 small shallot, minced

2 tablespoons balsamic vinegar, or to taste

2 teaspoons maple syrup, or to taste

1 teaspoon Dijon mustard

1 cup (150g) cherry tomatoes, halved

Not one but two editors call this salad their favorite recipe on all of Food52. If you must know more, it's a tumble of sweet, mellow roasted radicchio, tomatoes, and shrimp that takes all of twenty minutes to pull off. Balsamic-bathed radicchio roast just to the point of collapse, while a pan of shrimp cook almost instantly in the same oven. Up on the stove, a bacon vinaigrette simmers, a little sweet with even more balsamic. Opting for an aged vinegar will guard against additional bitterness, but a touch more maple syrup will mellow things out in a pinch.

1. Position oven racks in the top and lower thirds of the oven. Heat the oven to 425°F (220°C).

2. In a large bowl, gently toss the radicchio wedges with 2 tablespoons of the olive oil, the vinegar, 1 teaspoon salt, and ¼ teaspoon pepper. Place the wedges, cut side down, in a baking dish that's just big enough to fit them snugly. Let the radicchio marinate at room temperature while the oven heats.

3. In a large bowl, toss the shrimp with the remaining tablespoon of olive oil, ¼ teaspoon salt, and ¼ teaspoon pepper. Spread into a single layer on a parchment-lined baking sheet.

4. Roast the radicchio, turning once, until tender and the leaves start to caramelize and crisp around the edges, about 15 minutes. When the radicchio is almost done, put the shrimp in the oven and roast until pink and firm, 3 to 5 minutes. Transfer the radicchio to a cutting board and chop into bite-size pieces, then combine with the shrimp in a large bowl.

5. To make the vinaigrette, in a large skillet, heat the olive oil over medium heat for 1 minute. Add the bacon and cook, stirring every so often, until the fat renders and the bacon starts to crisp, about 5 minutes. Add the shallot and cook just until softened and warmed through, a minute more. Off the heat, stir in the vinegar, maple syrup, and mustard, followed by the tomatoes. Taste the vinaigrette on a piece of your roasted radicchio; let its level of bitterness guide if you need more balsamic or maple syrup in your vinaigrette.

6. Pour the vinaigrette over the radicchio and shrimp and toss until evenly coated. Scatter the parsley over and serve warm or at room temperature.

Grilled Lobster Salad with Lemon-Thyme Butter

Grilled seafood + grilled citrus + avocado + spicy, citrusy, melty butter

Serves 2 | From Christine Burns Rudalevige

1 (2-pound/900g) live lobster

Chile oil, for brushing

1 lemon, quartered

½ cup (110g) unsalted butter

1 tablespoon fresh thyme leaves, minced

1½ teaspoons freshly squeezed lemon juice

Your favorite hot sauce

Kosher salt

½ ripe avocado, diced

Even though she lives in Maine, Christine Burns Rudalevige, a longtime Food52 contributor, prefers butter-bathed, Connecticut-style lobster rolls to Maine's mayo version. So sometimes she riffs on it with this salad, which takes the lobsters to the grill, adds a heavy hit of lemon, and tosses in some avocado for even more butteriness. You could serve the warm salad the lobster-roll way—on pillowy potato rolls. It'd also be mighty fine on a toasted slice of brioche or a bed of crisp lettuce. Or chop everything (including the grilled lemons) to scoop up with tortilla chips.

1. Parcook your lobster in a large pot of boiling water that's as salty as the sea. Hold on to the lobster by the smooth part of the body and quickly drop it, head first, into the water. Cover and cook for 8 to 10 minutes.

2. Remove the lobster with tongs and let cool until you can handle it easily. Then, turn it on its back and, using a really sharp knife, slice it lengthwise down the center. (Remove the soft greenish paste that will ooze out.) Take a meat mallet and give each claw a good whack so they crack slightly. Brush the exposed flesh and shell with chile oil. Do the same to the lemon quarters.

3. Heat the grill to high and brush your grates clean. While the grill heats up, melt the butter over low heat without stirring. Skim off the milky solids at the top with a spoon so you're just left with the golden, clarified fat underneath. Stir in the thyme, lemon juice, and a squirt of hot sauce and season with salt. Set the clarified butter aside, but keep it warm.

4. When the grill is hot, place the lemon quarters and the lobster halves on the grate, exposed flesh down. Cook the lobsters, untouched, for 6 to 7 minutes. Cook the lemon until slightly charred, just a couple minutes.

5. When the lobster is done, work quickly to remove the tail, claw, and leg meat and cut it all into bite-size pieces. Mix the meat with 2 tablespoons of the clarified butter. You can mix in more if you like, but you want the meat to be dressed, not drowning. Gingerly mix in the avocado. Serve warm, with the grilled lemon squeezed over.

Seared Scallop Salad with Black Lentils & Garlic-Sesame Crumbs

Seared protein + lentils + dainty greens + breadcrumbs + zesty dressing

Serves 4 | From Emily Connor

1½ cups (285g) beluga lentils, rinsed and picked over

1 bay leaf

5 tablespoons (75ml) vegetable or neutral-flavored oil

5 garlic cloves, peeled and smashed

½ cup (30g) panko breadcrumbs

2 tablespoons white sesame seeds

Kosher salt and freshly ground black pepper

12 to 16 large scallops (about 1 pound/450g), muscle removed, rinsed, and dried well

1 cup (20g) loosely packed fresh cilantro leaves

4 cups (180g) firmly packed microgreens

Lemon-Ginger Dressing

2 teaspoons finely grated fresh ginger

2 tablespoons freshly squeezed lemon juice, plus more as needed

1 tablespoon rice vinegar

2 teaspoons sesame oil

3 tablespoons vegetable or other neutral oil

Kosher salt and freshly ground black pepper

Black, pearly lentils serve as the springboard for a salad that's jumpy with attention grabbers: seared scallops, a sesame-spiked ginger dressing, garlicky breadcrumbs and sesame seeds, and wisps of herbs and microgreens. It's an elegant affair that, aside from the scallops, can be made several hours in advance and held at room temperature until guests arrive. Go ahead and sneak some handfuls of those garlic-sesame breadcrumbs, though.

1. In a saucepan, bring the lentils, 6 cups (1.4L) water, and the bay leaf to a boil. Turn down the heat and gently simmer until the lentils are tender but not mushy, 15 to 20 minutes.

2. To make the dressing, in a bowl, whisk together the ginger, lemon juice, rice vinegar, sesame oil, and vegetable oil until emulsified. Taste and adjust the seasoning with salt, pepper, and more lemon juice.

3. In a small nonstick skillet, warm 2 tablespoons of the vegetable oil and the garlic over low heat; you want to hear the garlic faintly sizzle. Cook, turning several times, until light brown, about 5 minutes; remove the garlic from the oil and discard. Add the panko and sesame seeds to the garlic oil, stirring well to evenly coat. Turn the heat to medium and cook, stirring often, until the panko is crispy and the sesame seeds are golden brown. Off the heat, season with salt.

4. Drain the lentils and transfer to a large bowl, discarding the bay leaf. Immediately toss the lentils with about half of the dressing and season with salt. Set aside to cool.

5. Season the scallops with salt and pepper. In a 12-inch (30cm) skillet, heat the remaining 3 tablespoons of vegetable oil over medium-high heat. When the oil shimmers, arrange the scallops in a single layer, working in batches if needed. Cook the scallops, undisturbed, until golden brown, 1 to 2 minutes. Flip and sear them on the second side until just cooked through, 1 to 2 minutes more.

6. Stir the cilantro and microgreens into the cooled lentils and drizzle with enough dressing to evenly coat. Place on a large serving platter or individual plates. Top with the scallops, shower with the garlic-sesame crumbs, and serve right away.

Fresh Corn Cakes with Crab-Tomato Salad

Cakes/patties/burgers + fresh salad on top

Serves 4 | From Caroline Wright

4 cups (620g) fresh corn kernels (from 4 ears) or thawed frozen kernels

2 eggs

¼ cup (60ml) sour cream

Kosher salt and freshly ground black pepper

2 scallions, chopped, white and green parts separate

½ cup (60g) cornmeal

¼ cup (30g) all-purpose flour

5 tablespoons (75ml) olive oil

1 teaspoon white wine vinegar

1 pound (450g) tomatoes, cut into ½-inch (1.3cm) pieces

8 ounces (225g) fresh cooked crabmeat, picked over for shells

¼ cup (5g) loosely packed fresh basil leaves, torn if large

These shallow-fried corn cakes—crisp around the edges, tangy from sour cream, with corn-kernel jewels throughout—are so good hot from the pan you'll have to guard them against uninvited "tasters." But not for long. Since you mix the crab and tomato with scallions and a simple vinaigrette while the corn cakes are sizzling, there's no waiting around to speak of. Fry only as many corn cakes as you need and refrigerate any unused batter for a day or two so you can turn them out fresh.

1. Blend 2 cups (310g) of the corn, the eggs, and sour cream until smooth. Transfer to a large bowl, season with salt and pepper, and stir in the remaining 2 cups (310g) corn, the scallion whites, cornmeal, and flour just until combined.

2. In a large skillet, heat ¼ cup (60ml) of the olive oil over medium-high heat. Working in batches, spoon ¼ cupfuls (60ml) of the corn batter into the skillet and pat to flatten into small cakes. Cook, flipping once, until golden on both sides, about 3 minutes per side.

3. While the corn cakes cook, in a large bowl, stir together the remaining tablespoon of olive oil and the vinegar. Fold in the tomatoes, crab, and scallion greens and season with salt and pepper.

4. When all of the corn cakes are cooked, add the basil to the crab and tomato mixture and toss together until evenly coated. Divide the corn cakes among 4 plates, spoon the crab salad over the top, and serve.

How to Get Corn Off Its Cob Easily

This way of denuding an ear of corn probably seems really obvious, but once you see how few kernels go flying, you'll be happy creative director Kristen Miglore passed along this good tip. Lay a shucked ear of corn flat on your cutting board, with the pointy end facing away from you. Using a very sharp knife, slice off a strip of kernels down one side of the ear. Turn the ear so it's lying on the flat strip you've just created, and slice another strip of kernels off the cob. Keep rotating the ear until you've removed all the kernels.

Halibut Escabeche Taco Salad

Fried marinated fish + crunch + creamy sauce

Serves 4 | From Emily Connor

Halibut Escabeche

1½ pounds (680g) halibut, cod, or other white fish fillets

Kosher salt and freshly ground black pepper

Wondra or all-purpose flour, for dusting

¾ cup (175ml) olive oil

1 sweet onion (such as Vidalia or Walla Walla), thinly sliced

4 fat garlic cloves, thinly sliced

1 poblano pepper, stemmed, seeded, and thinly sliced

1 bay leaf

1½ teaspoons cumin seeds

¾ cup (175ml) white wine vinegar

½ cup (120ml) sour cream

2 teaspoons finely chopped canned chipotle chile in adobo sauce, or to taste

1 to 2 tablespoons freshly squeezed lime juice

2 tablespoons olive oil

2 small flour or corn tortillas, cut into strips

½ head savoy cabbage

1 watermelon radish

1 ripe avocado

Juice of 1 lime

1 cup (20g) loosely packed fresh cilantro leaves

Spanish escabeche sounds much more highbrow than it actually is: It's like ceviche but with fried, instead of raw, fish. Already, it sounds great, right? To develop the recipe here, Emily turned to one in *Fish Without a Doubt* by Rick Moonen, which takes care to not let the vinegar overpower the delicate fish. The rest of the salad does the same. Lots of fresh ingredients, fried tortilla (though store-bought tortilla chips could totally be used), and everything's tied together with an addictive chipotle-lime crema. Because most of the work is done a day in advance, you can spend the afternoon at the beach and "throw" this salad together for dinner. Nothing fussy about that.

1. To make the escabeche, season the fish with salt and pepper, then dust with Wondra flour to lightly and evenly coat. In a 12-inch (30cm) skillet, heat ¼ cup (60ml) of the olive oil over medium-high heat until it shimmers. Fry the fish until it's light golden on one side, 2 to 3 minutes, then flip and fry until nearly cooked through, 1 to 2 minutes more. Transfer the fish to a nonreactive glass or ceramic container.

2. In a separate skillet, heat ¼ cup (60ml) of the olive oil over medium heat. Sauté the onion, garlic, poblano, bay leaf, and cumin seeds until the onion and poblano soften but don't color, about 5 minutes. Season with salt. Pour in the vinegar and ¾ cup (175ml) water and turn the heat to high. Once at a vigorous boil, pour the vinegar mixture over the fish, followed by the remaining ¼ cup (60ml) olive oil. Press down gently to submerge the fish. Let cool to room temperature, then cover and refrigerate at least 8 hours, or up to a day. Let come to room temperature before serving.

3. To make the crema, stir together the sour cream, chipotle, and lime juice. Taste and add more adobo sauce, if you like. (The crema will keep in an airtight container in the refrigerator for up to 3 days.)

4. To make the tortilla strips, heat the olive oil over medium-high heat. Fry the tortilla strips, stirring occasionally, until crispy on both sides, 3 to 5 minutes. Transfer to a paper towel–lined plate to drain.

5. Thinly slice the cabbage, radish, and avocado. Toss the cabbage with 2 tablespoons of the halibut marinade and the lime juice, followed by the radish, avocado, and cilantro. Break the fish into large flakes and gently fold them in, adding more marinade if the salad looks dry. Transfer to a platter or plates and drizzle with the crema. Serve immediately.

Herbed Tuna & Israeli Couscous Salad

Protein + pasta or grain + chopped herbs + spiced oil + citrus

Serves 4 | From Jennifer Engle

2 teaspoons cumin seeds

1 teaspoon coriander seeds

⅓ cup (80ml) extra-virgin olive oil

1 teaspoon cayenne pepper

Kosher salt

2 cups (340g) Israeli couscous

1 (8.81-ounce/250g) can olive oil–packed tuna (such as Ortiz Bonito del Norte), mostly drained and broken into chunks

Juice from ½ orange

1 cup (20g) loosely packed fresh cilantro leaves, coarsely chopped

1 cup (20g) loosely packed fresh flat-leaf parsley leaves, coarsely chopped

2 to 3 tablespoons minced preserved lemon rind, rinsed

1 tablespoon freshly squeezed lemon juice

Not to be confused with the canned tuna of childhood sandwiches, the oil-packed variety is flaky, flavorful, and the saving grace of many a weekday meal. But while a can of fish does not an entire dinner make, add it to a couscous (or quinoa—you know you want to) salad that's spicy, with spunk from preserved lemon and mellow sweetness from orange juice, and you need little else.

1. In a dry skillet, toast the cumin and coriander seeds over medium heat until fragrant, tossing the pan to prevent burning. Transfer to a mortar, then turn off the heat but return the skillet to burner. Carefully pour the olive oil into the hot skillet.

2. Using the mortar and pestle, crush the toasted spices into a powder. Transfer the hot oil to a large serving bowl, followed by the crushed spices and cayenne.

3. Bring a large pot of generously salted water to a boil. Add the couscous and cook until tender and liquid is absorbed, 8 to 10 minutes. Drain in a colander.

4. Add the tuna and half the orange juice to the spiced oil. Fold in the couscous, followed by the cilantro and parsley. Toss with the remaining orange juice to combine. Fold in 2 tablespoons of the preserved lemon and the lemon juice. Taste and adjust the seasoning with salt and the remaining preserved lemon. Eat right away, or cover and refrigerate for up to a day. Let the salad come to room temperature before serving.

Preserve Your Own Lemons

———————

Whereas fresh lemon tickles your nose, preserved lemon uppercuts, delivering a sweet-salty hit to any dish it graces (in many ways, like capers). To make your own, scrub lemons with a vegetable brush really well. Quarter a lemon, keeping the bottom half or so uncut so it resembles a flower. Fill the center with a big pinch of kosher salt. Plop the lemon into a mason jar, cover it with another sprinkle of salt, and repeat until your jar is really full. Pack the lemons in so they start to lose some of their liquid; squeeze in juice if they're not already covered. Seal the jar and let the lemons hang out on your counter for two or three weeks. They're ready when the skins look pliable, like you want to eat them! Once the jar is opened, the preserved lemons will keep in the fridge for up to a year—their flavor will diminish as time goes on.

Salmon & Beet Salad
with Cherry Vinaigrette

Roots + fish + spicy leaves + stone fruit + sweet vinaigrette

Serves 4 | From Emily Connor

4 large red beets

Olive oil, for roasting

Kosher salt and freshly
ground black pepper

1 pound (450g) salmon
fillets, preferably about
1 inch (2.5cm) thick

6 cups (120g) loosely
packed baby arugula
leaves, or mixture of
arugula and watercress

½ to ¾ cup (80 to 115g)
sweet cherries, pitted
and chopped

¼ cup (35g) roasted
almonds, coarsely
chopped

3 tablespoons torn
fresh mint

Cherry Vinaigrette

About 5 sweet
cherries, pitted

2 tablespoons
minced shallots

2 tablespoons
sherry vinegar

1 tablespoon
balsamic vinegar

Kosher salt and freshly
ground black pepper

7 tablespoons (105ml)
extra-virgin olive oil

Like grapes and cheddar (page 135), beets and cherries belong with each other in unsuspected ways. Their moody, bleeding stains run together, the earthiness of roasted beets grounding the sweet, sweet cherry. Add salmon (baked here, because the oven's already on, but grilled works, too), and you've got a pretty spectrum of pinkish reds but also a main-course salad. The arugula keeps things light, though to make the dish fully in advance, use a sturdier green like thin ribbons of kale.

1. Heat the oven to 400°F (200°C). Trim the beets and scrub if they're dirty. Lay a large piece of aluminum foil on a baking sheet, place the beets in the center, and coat with olive oil, salt, and pepper. Fold the foil to make a packet and crimp the edges. Bake until tender (you can check by piercing a fork through the foil), 45 to 60 minutes, depending on their size. Remove from the oven but leave the oven on. When cool enough to handle, remove them from the foil, peel off the skin, and coarsely chop.

2. While the beets roast, make the vinaigrette. Use a mortar and pestle to pound the cherries to a coarse purée, or pulse in a mini food processor. Transfer to a small bowl, then add the shallots, sherry and balsamic vinegars, and a pinch of salt. Gradually whisk in the olive oil until emulsified. Taste and adjust seasoning with more salt, pepper, or vinegar. (The vinaigrette will keep in an airtight container in the refrigerator for up to 3 days; bring to room temp before using.)

3. Place the salmon on a parchment-lined baking sheet, season with salt and pepper, and coat with 1 to 2 tablespoons of the cherry vinaigrette. Roast until the salmon is cooked to your liking, 10 to 15 minutes for medium. Remove from the oven, let cool, and then flake into large pieces.

4. In a large bowl, toss together the arugula with just enough of the vinaigrette to lightly coat the leaves. Then, gently fold in the chopped cherries, beets, almonds, and mint. Arrange the salad on a large platter, nestle in the salmon, and serve.

Shrimp Ceviche with Caramelized Tangerine Vinaigrette

Marinated seafood + lots of citrus + delicate herbs + chile

Serves 4 | From Emily Connor

1 pound (450g) medium shrimp, peeled, deveined, and tails removed, or scallops or a firm white fish

1 jalapeño or Fresno chile, or to taste

2 Persian cucumbers

4 satsuma tangerines or 1 large sumo tangerine

½ cup (25g) firmly packed dill leaves

1 large ripe avocado

Kosher salt

Caramelized Tangerine Vinaigrette

4 satsuma tangerines or 1 large sumo tangerine

¼ cup (60ml) extra-virgin olive oil, plus more as needed

2 tablespoons sugar

2 teaspoons sherry vinegar, plus more as needed

Kosher salt

In a ceviche, you expect the citrus (typically lime) to be screaming above the other ingredients—zesty, bright, look at me! But here, tangerine has a nicer streak so the focus swerves to the shrimp, avocado, chile, and cucumber. Not only do slices of tangerine sweeten the jumble, but sugar-crusted halves are caramelized and juiced for a mellow, more supportive vinaigrette. This riff on an Amanda Hesser creation, which also works with grapefruit and blood oranges, goes great on salads with tender ingredients like asparagus or baby lettuces, but will shy in the face of kale and roasted vegetables.

1. Bring 4 quarts (3.8L) of generously salted water to a boil in a large pot. Add the shrimp and cook until opaque, 1 to 2 minutes. Transfer the shrimp with a slotted spoon to an ice bath.

2. To make the vinaigrette, zest the tangerine and then cut in half crosswise. Place the zest and sugar in separate small bowls. In a nonstick sauté pan, lightly coat the bottom of the pan with olive oil over medium-high heat. Dip the cut side of each tangerine half in the sugar to lightly and thoroughly coat. When the pan is hot, press the sugared tangerine halves onto the pan and let bubble and sizzle until lightly caramelized, 2 to 3 minutes. Check them often to avoid blackening. Transfer to a plate.

3. Once the tangerine halves are cool enough to handle, squeeze their juice (should be about ¼ cup/60ml) over the zest. Whisk in the sherry vinegar and ¼ cup (60ml) olive oil and season with salt. Taste and adjust the seasoning with salt and vinegar.

4. Drain the shrimp and transfer to a shallow glass or ceramic dish. Add all but 2 tablespoons of the vinaigrette to the shrimp and toss to evenly coat; cover and marinate in the refrigerator for 30 to 60 minutes.

5. Meanwhile, thinly slice the chile into rings, cut the cucumbers on the diagonal into ¼-inch (6mm) slices, peel and cut the tangerine into supremes or thin slices, coarsely chop the dill, and thinly slice the avocado.

6. Just before serving, transfer the shrimp with a slotted spoon to a serving bowl or platter. Stir in the chile and cucumbers, then gently fold in the tangerine, dill, and avocado with the remaining vinaigrette. Season with salt. Serve cold or at room temperature.

Meat Salads

Chicken & Rice Salad with Poached Radishes and Nuoc Cham

Shredded meat + spicy greens + grains + brown butter + heat

Serves 4 | From Ali Slagle

2 tablespoons unsalted butter

12 radishes, cleaned, trimmed, and quartered, or halved if they're tiny

Kosher salt and freshly ground black pepper

2 cups (40g) loosely packed watercress, baby kale, or other spicy green

1½ cups (210g) shredded chicken

1 cup (200g) cooked long-grain brown rice

1 cup (40g) chopped fresh cilantro leaves and stems

Nuoc Cham

3 tablespoons fish sauce

1 tablespoon freshly grated lime zest

3 tablespoons freshly squeezed lime juice

2 tablespoons sugar, plus more as needed

1 garlic clove, sliced

2 Thai chiles, halved lengthwise and sliced into half-moons

Freshly ground black pepper

It all starts with the radishes—seared, then poached in brown butter. You could add some baby kale and acid and stop there, but keep following along. Add nuoc cham, which really is a puckery Vietnamese dipping sauce made from fish sauce and lime juice. Warmed by the radishes and butter, it's rendered round, substantial. Chicken (rotisserie chicken from the store is a great option) and rice then happily join in, and the whole thing gets heaped on wisps and doodles of spicy greens and cilantro and their stems (yes, you want the stems). When our books editor cobbled this recipe together with ideas from blogger Sarah Britton, as well as Merrill's mom and Momofuku, she wanted to keep adding ingredients—sesame seeds, sprouts, orange slices—but resisted before things got unruly. The solution: just make it again.

1. To make the nuoc cham, combine the fish sauce, lime zest and juice, and sugar in a jar, seal, and shake until the sugar is completely dissolved. Stir in the garlic, chiles, and a few grinds of pepper, then let everything hang out for around 30 minutes (you can eat the nuoc cham immediately, but the flavors won't be as developed). Taste and adjust the seasoning if needed (if it's too puckery, add more sugar). The nuoc cham will keep in its jar in the fridge for up to a week.

2. In a large skillet, melt the butter over medium-low heat. Add the radishes, cut side down, and a pinch of salt and sauté until tender and slightly browned, about 10 minutes.

3. In the meantime, scatter the watercress on a serving platter.

4. When the radishes are ready, add 3 tablespoons of the nuoc cham, and stir to coat the radishes. Stir in the chicken and brown rice. Immediately pour the mixture over the greens, drizzling the nuoc cham all over.

5. Gently toss together just to coat the leaves. Taste and add more nuoc cham, if you like. Sprinkle the cilantro over the top and serve immediately.

Chorizo & Summer Melon Salad

Spicy cured meat + melon + crisp vegetables + crumbly cheese + herbs + citrus

Serves 4 | From Emily Connor

1½ cups (235g) cubed cantaloupe or watermelon

4 ounces (115g) dried Spanish chorizo, cut into ⅛-inch (3mm) slices

1 cup (150g) cherry tomatoes, halved

1 cup (105g) thinly sliced cucumber

Sea salt

3 tablespoons extra-virgin olive oil

2 tablespoons freshly squeezed lemon juice, or to taste

½ cup (75g) crumbled feta

¼ cup (5g) loosely packed fresh mint leaves, torn if large

Smoky cured chorizo has a way of turning a summery salad downright feisty; its spices sneak out into the vinaigrette while the slices soften and fold. Factor in rounds of cucumber, tiny cubes of cantaloupe, and tomatoes, feta, and mint, and this no-cook salad is practically spoonable. Ladle it next to grilled fish, shrimp, crusty bread—even black beans, or right from the tub.

1. In a large bowl, combine the cantaloupe, chorizo, tomatoes, and cucumber. Sprinkle with a few pinches of salt and toss together.

2. Add the olive oil and lemon juice and toss again. Fold in the feta and mint. Taste and adjust with salt and lemon juice until the flavors pop.

3. Set aside at room temperature for at least 5 minutes, or up to an hour, to let the flavors meld. (The salad will keep in an airtight container in the refrigerator for up to 4 hours; for the best results, let sit at room temp for 10 to 15 minutes and add the tomatoes and mint just before serving.)

Genius Tip: Chorizo—You Can Pickle That

When the brainiacs behind the blog *Ideas in Food*, H. Alexander Talbot and Aki Kamozawa, tell you to pickle chorizo, your face might contort just thinking about all the spice and vinegar and *pow*. But their way is more strategic than chaotic, combining 5 tablespoons (75ml) each of soy sauce and balsamic, sherry, and rice vinegars with 8 ounces (225g) thinly sliced dried Spanish chorizo in a sterilized jar. After refrigerating for 2 days, you have sweetened chorizo *and* a potent liquid that's revving up for a full-throttle vinaigrette. Use the pickled pieces or a dressing made of their by-products in a salad with roasted vegetables (page 43), earthy grains (page 73), or seafood (page 115). The chorizo would also not be out of place on top of stew, beans, sautéed greens, or a baked potato. The pickled chorizo keeps in the fridge for up to forever.

Steak & Tossed Salsa Verde Salad

Grilled steak and alliums + greens + nuts/herbs/cheese + garlicky vinaigrette

Serves 4 | From Emily Connor

1½ pounds (680g) hanger or flank steak

Kosher salt and freshly ground black pepper

Olive oil, for brushing

1 large red onion, cut crosswise into ½-inch (1.3cm) rounds

6 cups (120g) loosely packed watercress and arugula leaves

¼ cup (5g) loosely packed fresh flat-leaf parsley leaves

¼ cup (10g) loosely packed fresh mint leaves, torn if large

½ cup (50g) toasted walnuts, coarsely chopped

2 ounces (55g) Parmesan, shaved with a vegetable peeler

Lemon-Anchovy Vinaigrette

1 garlic clove

2 anchovy fillets

Grated zest of 2 lemons

3 tablespoons freshly squeezed lemon juice

2 teaspoons capers, coarsely chopped

½ teaspoon Dijon mustard

Pinch of red pepper flakes, or to taste

¼ cup (60ml) extra-virgin olive oil

Here's a salad to make grillside, with a glass of rosé in one hand. Instead of whirring up an Italian salsa verde with summer's sprightly herbs and spicy greens, use them as the salad's greens. Salsa verde's other piquant ingredients—anchovies, garlic, lemon, and capers—dress the greens, steak, and some charred red onions. Now, where'd that rosé bottle go?

1. Pat the steak dry with paper towels, generously season with salt, and let sit at room temperature for an hour.

2. Heat the grill to medium-high heat and brush your grates clean. Lightly brush the steak on both sides with olive oil. Brush the onion with olive oil and season with salt and pepper.

3. Grill the steak and onion until the onion is nicely charred and the steak's cooked to your desired doneness, 3 to 5 minutes per side (for medium-rare, the internal temperature should reach 130°F/55°C). Transfer the steak to a cutting board and the onion to a plate. Let the steak rest for about 15 minutes, then thinly slice across the grain.

4. To make the vinaigrette, finely chop and smash the garlic and anchovies into a paste with the side of your knife. In a large bowl, whisk together the lemon zest and juice, capers, mustard, red pepper flakes, and olive oil until emulsified. Taste and adjust the seasoning.

5. On a large serving platter or in a bowl, combine the watercress, arugula, parsley, mint, walnuts, and Parmesan. Add the vinaigrette, a little at a time, and toss with your hands to lightly dress the salad. Top the greens with the sliced steak and onion. Serve with the remaining vinaigrette on the side.

Grilled Cheese Croutons

A grilled cheese cut into crouton-size cubes can go where sandwiches haven't gone (throughout your salad, for one) and can do what a full-size one just can't—or shouldn't. While you may love a stinky or blue cheese, eating a whole grilled cheese of it can be a lot to handle. But make that sandwich (layer on some sautéed onions, apples, or bacon, while you're at it), then cut it into smaller-than-bite-size cubes or triangles, and you have multilayered croutons for your every hearty salad.

Bloody Mary Steak Salad

Grilled meat + crunchy veg + briny, salty, spicy

Serves 4 | From Ali Slagle

1½ pounds (680g) skirt or hanger steak

1 tablespoon sherry vinegar

1 tablespoon balsamic vinegar

Juice of 1 lemon

2 tablespoons prepared horseradish

1 tablespoon Worcestershire sauce

1½ teaspoons of your favorite hot sauce

2 cups (300g) cherry tomatoes, halved

½ cup (60g) thinly sliced red onion

½ cup (50g) sliced celery, cut into thin half-moons, plus some leaves if you'd like

¼ cup (35g) chopped briny green olives, plus 2 tablespoons olive brine

2 tablespoons pickled jalapeños

Freshly ground black pepper

¼ cup (35g) crumbled blue cheese

½ cup (10g) loosely packed fresh flat-leaf parsley leaves

Bloody Marys and their garnishes are not tame specimens—or, rather, they shouldn't be—so a salad rendition(!) needs to follow suit. Because the skirt steak gets grilled naked and then marinated after the fact, the boisterous ingredients (pickles, horseradish, hot sauce, and friends) drive into the steak instead of shimmy around it. Edit or add garnishes based on what you like to balance atop your drink. Any which way, the result (reminiscent of Thai beef salad) isn't shy—both at room temperature but also warmed with some eggs for a steak-and-eggs situation. And go ahead, serve it with a Bloody Mary.

1. Heat the grill to medium-high and brush your grates clean, or heat a grill pan over high heat on the stove top. Grill the unseasoned steak until browned well on both sides and cooked to your desired doneness, 3 to 4 minutes per side for medium-rare (the internal temperature should reach 130°F/55°C). Transfer the steak to a cutting board and let rest while you prepare the remaining ingredients.

2. In a large bowl, whisk together both vinegars, the lemon juice, horseradish, Worcestershire, and hot sauce. Stir in the tomatoes, onion, celery, olives and brine, and jalapeños. Grind a good amount of pepper over the top and stir.

3. Cut the meat across the grain into ½-inch (1.3cm) slices and mix into the salad. Marinate for at least 30 minutes, or up to 3 days.

4. Stir in the blue cheese, parsley, and celery leaves and serve.

A Speedy Way to Slice Little Tomatoes

Slicing slippery little tomato after slippery tomato can get as labor-intensive as pitting olives (page 90), or picking herbs off their stems (page 10)—but we've got a trick! Grab the lids from two plastic containers, and place one, right side up, on your counter. Fill it with a layer of tomatoes. Place the other lid, upside down, on top of the tomatoes. Gently press down with your nondominant hand to keep the little dudes in place. With the serrated knife in your other hand, gingerly slice through the tomatoes. Continue throughout all of tomato season.

Spicy Chicken Salad with Rice Noodles

Grilled meat + thinly sliced veg + noodles + herbs + citrusy-spicy dressing

Serves 4 | From Merrill Stubbs

1½ tablespoons lime juice

2 tablespoons fish sauce

1 tablespoon light brown sugar

2 teaspoons chile-garlic sauce

1 teaspoon sriracha

2 garlic cloves, peeled and crushed

6 skin-on, bone-in chicken thighs

2 cups (140g) shredded savoy cabbage

1 cup (110g) julienned carrots

1 cup (80g) thinly sliced sugar snap peas

1 red bell pepper, seeded and thinly sliced

3 scallions, thinly sliced

1 jalapeño, thinly sliced

Sea salt

8 ounces (225g) pad thai rice noodles

Handful of basil and mint leaves, coarsely chopped

Lime-Sriracha Dressing

6 tablespoons (90ml) walnut oil

⅓ cup (80ml) lime juice

5 tablespoons (75ml) fish sauce

1 tablespoon toasted sesame oil

1 tablespoon rice vinegar

1 tablespoon light brown sugar

2 teaspoons sriracha

1 garlic clove, minced

½ teaspoon sea salt

This salad of bouncy noodles has charred chicken peeking through the loops—along with a whole lot of tricks. What your other salads can learn is that bone-in chicken thighs can be blackened and the meat pulled right off, so rich it couldn't possibly be chicken; that gutsy fish sauce can turn sweet and nutty with a little help from friends; that rice noodles will resist mushiness after a rinse in cold water. The only other secret is the julienned vegetables, which disappear into the tangle like blades of grass.

1. In a wide shallow bowl, stir together the lime juice, fish sauce, brown sugar, chile-garlic sauce, sriracha, and garlic. Add the chicken and turn to coat thoroughly and evenly. Cover and marinate in the fridge for 3 to 6 hours.

2. In a large bowl, toss together the cabbage, carrots, sugar snap peas, bell pepper, scallions, jalapeño, and a couple pinches of salt.

3. To make the dressing, whisk together all the ingredients. Taste and adjust the seasoning.

4. Let the chicken come to room temperature. Bring a large pot of generously salted water to a boil. When the water boils, cook the noodles according to the package directions. Drain under cold running water for a minute or two. Drain again and add to the vegetables.

5. Heat a grill or grill pan to medium heat. Remove the chicken thighs from the marinade, letting any excess drip back into the bowl, and sprinkle each lightly with salt on all sides. Cook the thighs, fat side down, on the grill until the fat is crisp and charred, about 7 minutes. Flip the thighs and grill until cooked through, 5 to 7 minutes more. To check for doneness, slice into a thigh to make sure that there isn't any pink remaining. Remove from the grill. When the thighs are cool enough to handle, cut the meat off the bones and then slice it crosswise, so that each slice includes a little strip of charred, crispy fat.

6. Toss the vegetables and noodles with about two-thirds of the dressing. Taste and add more dressing if you like. Fold in the chicken, basil, and mint, and serve.

Grilled Lamb Kebabs with Tomato-Cucumber Salad

Kebabs + vegetable chunks + herbs + yogurt dressing

Serves 4 | From Emily Connor

1½ cups (355ml) full-fat plain yogurt

3 tablespoons extra-virgin olive oil, plus more for drizzling

1 tablespoon minced garlic

1 teaspoon minced fresh rosemary

½ teaspoon Aleppo pepper or red pepper flakes

Grated zest of 1 lemon

2 tablespoons freshly squeezed lemon juice, plus more for drizzling

2 pounds (900g) boneless leg of lamb, trimmed and cut into 2-inch (5cm) chunks

Kosher salt

2 cups (300g) cherry tomatoes, halved

3 Persian cucumbers, thinly sliced

1 tablespoon tahini, stirred in the jar

Handful of fresh flat-leaf parsley leaves or mint, chopped

Every good recipe is also a launching pad, and because this one has a few components that go really well together, it's a moment to spring forth and make it your own way. Make it a leafier salad with lots of whole herbs, finely dice the cucumbers for more of a relish, serve the sauce as a dip or coat the vegetables with it (a dressing is a sauce, basically—see page 70). Nestle the kebabs with other salads, like grilled corn and barley (page 35) or lemon-dill orzo (page 90). Eat it all up in a pita, or swirled through grains. You thought you were only getting one salad out of this, didn't you?

1. In a wide, shallow bowl, stir together 1 cup (240ml) of the yogurt, the olive oil, garlic, rosemary, Aleppo, and lemon zest and juice.

2. Add the lamb and turn to coat the chunks thoroughly and evenly. Cover and refrigerate for at least 2 hours, or up to 24 hours. (The longer the meat marinates, the better it will be.)

3. Remove the lamb from the marinade, letting any excess drip off. Thread the lamb onto skewers, season generously with salt, and let stand at room temperature while the grill heats up.

4. Heat the grill to medium-high heat and brush your grates clean. Grill the lamb until cooked to your desired doneness, 4 to 5 minutes per side for medium-rare (the internal temperature should reach 140°F/60°C). Let the lamb rest for about 10 minutes.

5. Meanwhile, season the tomatoes with salt. In a colander set over the sink, salt the cucumbers to draw out the moisture.

6. In a small bowl, stir together the remaining ½ cup (115ml) of yogurt and the tahini and season with salt.

7. Just before serving, in a large bowl, stir together the tomatoes, cucumber (discarding any accumulated liquid), and parsley and drizzle with lemon juice and olive oil. Serve on a large platter with lamb kebabs—tahini yogurt on the side.

Curried Chicken, Grape & Cheddar Salad

Grilled meat and bread + curry + lettuce + fruit + hard cheese + vinegar

Serves 4 | From Emily Connor

1 tablespoon mild
curry powder

1 tablespoon plain yogurt

1 tablespoon olive oil

2 pounds (900g) skin-on
chicken thighs, bone-in
or boneless

Kosher salt and freshly
ground black pepper

3 (½-inch/1.3cm) slices
crusty bread (such as
ciabatta or sourdough)

3 tablespoons olive oil

2 small heads Bibb
lettuce, leaves separated

1 cup (150g) Concord,
Thomcords, or red
Thompson grapes,
halved and seeded

2 to 3 ounces (55 to 85g)
aged cheddar, crumbled
or cut into small pieces

Sherry Vinaigrette

¼ cup (60ml) extra-
virgin olive oil

2 tablespoons sherry
vinegar

Kosher salt and freshly
ground black pepper

When curried chicken, grapes, cheddar, and grilled bread get piled one by one onto Bibb lettuce, the soft leaves nestle all the apparently random ingredients together into one smart, if haphazard, dish. Emily got this idea from a similarly strange but good salad at a bistro in Paris—and we're sure glad she did. The chicken's marinade (equal parts curry powder, yogurt, and olive oil) is a good one to remember for other meats, and layering instead of tossing the ingredients means wispy and weighty ones can stay side by side in their ideal, uncrushed forms—ready for you to finagle perfect forkfuls.

1. In a small bowl, stir together the curry powder, yogurt, and olive oil. Rub the paste all over the chicken, making sure to get it under the skin. Transfer the chicken to a wide shallow bowl and let marinate in the refrigerator for a few hours, or up to overnight.

2. Remove the chicken from the refrigerator, season with salt, and let sit at room temperature for 1 hour.

3. Meanwhile, make the vinaigrette by whisking together the olive oil and vinegar. Season with salt and pepper.

4. Heat the grill to medium-high and brush your grates clean. Grill the chicken until the internal temperature reaches 165°F (75°C), about 5 minutes per side. Let the chicken rest for 10 minutes, then slice into ½-inch (1.3cm) slices.

5. Meanwhile, brush each slice of bread with olive oil, using just enough to coat each side. Season with a pinch of salt, and grill, checking it frequently, until charred in spots but soft in the center, a few minutes per side. Remove from the grill and, once cool, cut into ½-inch (1.3cm) cubes.

6. In a large bowl, toss the lettuce leaves with just enough of the vinaigrette to lightly coat and season with salt and pepper. On a serving platter or individual plates, layer the lettuce leaves with the chicken, grapes, cheddar, and bread. Serve immediately, passing the remaining vinaigrette at the table.

Slow-Roasted Duck & Apple Salad

Fall-apart tender meat + warm fruit + hearty greens + nuts + vinegar

Serves 2 | From Ginger's Kitchen

1 duck leg

Kosher salt and freshly ground pepper

2 tablespoons olive oil

½ sweet onion (such as Vidalia or Walla Walla)

2 Granny Smith apples

¼ cup (60ml) apple cider

¼ cup (60ml) Calvados or another brandy

4 fresh sage leaves

1 small bunch mustard greens

2 tablespoons unsalted butter

Good aged balsamic vinegar, for drizzling

¼ cup (30g) toasted pistachios

When Abbie Argersinger, Arielle Arizpe, Annaliese Bischoff, and Helen Morille—and dog, Ginger!—get together to cook, they call themselves Ginger's Kitchen, and great things happen. This salad is no exception. Practically speaking, it simplifies the process of cooking duck (low and slow in the oven) and puts fall apples to excellent use, but the real reason to make this is that it will take you to a picnic blanket somewhere close to Dijon. Make sure your mustard greens are spicy, and that someone brings the Sancerre, chilled.

1. Heat the oven to 250°F (120°C).

2. Generously season the duck leg with salt and pepper. In a skillet, heat the olive oil over medium heat. Cook the duck leg until browned on both sides, about 10 minutes, then transfer to a baking dish. Cut the onion and ½ apple into four wedges each and add to the baking dish. Pour the duck fat from the pan over everything, followed by the cider and Calvados. Lay the sage leaves on top, cover it all tightly with aluminum foil, and slide the baking dish into the oven for 2½ to 3 hours.

3. Searing the duck has probably completely destroyed your stove top with fat splatters—now's the time to clean up a bit. Also wash and trim your mustard greens and chop them into ½-inch (1.3cm) ribbons—keep them in the fridge until you need them again.

4. When the duck is completely fall-apart tender—to see if it's ready, give it a little poke with a fork—remove it from the oven.

5. In a griddle pan or sauté or cast-iron pan, melt the butter over medium-high heat. Cut the remaining 1½ apples into twelve wedges and griddle the wedges until they are just brown but not mushy, about 5 minutes per side.

6. Arrange the mustard greens on a platter. Remove the skin from the duck and use a fork to pull the meat away from the bone and shred it—be sure to avoid the tricky little bones that want to go along. Arrange the duck and apples on top of the greens, followed by the roasted onion and apple from the duck pan. Drizzle with a couple of tablespoons of pan drippings and the vinegar and sprinkle with the pistachios to serve.

Thai Pork Salad with Crisped Rice

Ground protein + crispy rice (maybe cereal) + lettuce bed + alliums

Serves 4 | From Emily Connor

2 tablespoons
vegetable oil

¾ cup (20g) crisped
rice cereal, such as
Rice Krispies

¼ teaspoon cayenne
pepper, or to taste

2 tablespoons fish sauce,
or to taste

Large pinch of sugar

1 pound (450g) ground
pork

4 garlic cloves, minced

3 fresh red Thai chiles
(or to taste), minced. or
a pinch of red pepper
flakes

1 shallot, thinly sliced

2 tablespoons freshly
squeezed lime juice, plus
more as needed

4 scallions, thinly sliced
on the diagonal

1 cup (20g) loosely
packed fresh cilantro
leaves, coarsely chopped

¼ cup (10g) fresh mint
leaves, coarsely chopped

1 large head Bibb lettuce,
or 2 to 3 heads Little
Gem lettuce, leaves
separated

2 Persian cucumbers or
½ English cucumber,
thinly sliced

A play on pork larb, this layered salad is everything you want from Thai food: bright, clean flavors, a heady depth from crispy pork bits and fish sauce, and heat that tickles rather than burns. Raw vegetables are there to play nice with the warm pork topping, and it's all topped off with quick-toasted, spicy Rice Krsipies that stands in for, and arguably bests, the toasted rice powder in traditional larb. Despite a long ingredient list, this dish comes together quickly and holds up well (just be sure to pack up the lettuce in a separate container). If you're not a pork person, swap in ground beef or chicken.

1. In a large nonstick skillet or a wok, heat 1 tablespoon of the vegetable oil over medium-high heat. Once the oil is shimmering, add the crisped rice cereal and cayenne and stir until browned just slightly, about 2 minutes, turning down the heat if necessary to prevent burning. Transfer to a bowl and wipe out the pan.

2. In a small bowl, stir together the fish sauce and sugar.

3. In the same skillet, heat the remaining tablespoon of vegetable oil over medium-high heat. Add the pork and cook, stirring frequently to break the meat into small pieces, until it is no longer pink, about 5 minutes. Add the garlic, chiles, and shallot, stirring to evenly distribute them with the pork, and continue to cook, pressing down firmly to help the pork brown and stirring just once or twice, until the pork is golden and crispy, 3 to 5 minutes. Drain and discard any excess oil. Stir in the fish sauce–sugar mixture and cook a few seconds longer to warm through. Off the heat, add 2 tablespoons of the lime juice. Taste and adjust the heat, acidity, and sweetness if needed. Let cool for about a minute, then toss in the scallions, cilantro, and mint.

4. On a large serving platter or plates, arrange a layer of lettuce leaves, then top with some of the pork mixture and cucumbers. Continue layering in the same way until you've used all of your ingredients. Scatter the crisped rice over the top. Serve immediately.

Thank Yous

To get here—to one cohesive book of stories, recipes, and tidbits about salad—it took a lot (*a lot*) of people's individual talents and ideas and opinions. Without any of these folks, the book would be missing a little flare. So for that:

Thank you, immensely, to EmilyC: We know your real name is Emily Connor, but we will always call you by your Food52 username. We measure all of our salads to the standards yours set, so getting thirty new recipes from you is like hitting the jackpot. We're grateful for your endless spunk, your excitement for this project, your enviable precision, and, simply, for making this process really fun.

Team Salad, also known as the Food52 editorial team (Kristen Miglore, Ali Slagle, Sarah Jampel, Kenzi Wilbur, Amanda Sims, Caroline Lange, Samantha Weiss-Hills, and Leslie Stephens): We've always managed to turn out pretty okay salads together with whatever's left in our respective fridges, so of course you wrote great headnotes and scouted great tips. Kristen and Sarah also know how to show off a salad's best sides—and style it before it wilts. They, too, are the soundboard and support system that kept Ali smiling as she kept this show on the road.

We're in awe of the creative cats James Ransom and Alexis Anthony, whose eagerness to try new things; commitment to telling a singular, beautiful story; and patience as the food stylists played with baby greens gave this book its dynamic feel. Alexis, your thoughtful art direction is apparent in every photo, and James, you're a magician (you know what we mean). Thank you also to the kitchen—Josh Cohen and his team Allison Buford, Scott Cavagnaro, Elena Apostolides, and Shannon Elliot—for cooking salad and not cooking it when the stylists wanted to, and to Carmen Ladipo, prop police and overall invaluable helping hand.

Thank you to Amanda and Merrill, for letting us do our salad thing in book form and encouraging us to have more fun and make bigger messes (within reason!!). And to the rest of the Food52 team, champions of not sad desk salads: It's all your under-the-hood work that lets this book be its best self. You are evidence that people do take care to make a salad, so we hope you buy this book for everyone you know! You, too, Amanda and Merrill.

To our troupe of testers, led by Stephanie Bourgeois—Angela Barros, Anna Francese Gass, Emily Olson, and Kate Knapp—thank you for treating salad like the precise science it isn't. Thank you also to CB Owens, proofing as precisely as the best.

Gratitude goes to everyone at Ten Speed Press, for knowing that salad is a topic deserving of a whole book and the center plate. It must be the Berkeley in you.

If it wasn't for our community, this book probably would've been exclusively quinoa, farro, and kale salads. These people are the ones who dreamt up salads so mighty, we crave them. Thank you for sharing your wisdom with us on Food52 and now in this book: Abbie Argersinger, Arielle Arizpe, Jeannine Balletto, Annaliese Bischoff, Mark Bittman, Nancy Brush, Christine Burns Rudalevige, Canal House, Josh Cohen, Dorie Colangelo, Emily Connor, Nicholas Day, Jennifer Engle, Sarah Fioritto, Phyllis Grant, Suzanne Goin, Emily Nichols Grossi, Shannon Hulley, Ideas in Food, Shruti Jain, Sarah Jampel, Sara Jenkins, Amanda Hesser, Catherine Lamb, Hunter Lewis, Paula Marchese, Kristen Miglore, Aleksandra Mojsilovic, Helen Morille, Ann Taylor Pittman, Barbara Reiss, Ali Slagle, Elizabeth Stark, Merrill Stubbs, Kenzi Wilbur, and Caroline Wright.

To show our appreciation, in a most fitting of ways, we made a recipe for you (we couldn't make a book without a dessert).

Berry Salad with Brioche Croutons (and a Side of Thank-You)

Heat the oven to 350°F (175°C). Cut 4 large slices of brioche into bite-size cubes. In a baking dish, combine the brioche with a handful of chopped nuts (almonds, walnuts, hazelnuts—your pick). Drizzle with 1 to 2 tablespoons of honey and sprinkle with sea salt. Bake until golden, about 7 minutes. Let cool, then store in an airtight container for up to 4 days. When you're ready for dessert, toss whatever berries you like with some raw sugar (that is the "dressing") and divide among 4 bowls. Top with the brioche croutons and be merry.

Index

Library of Congress Cataloging-in-Publication Data is
on file with the publisher.

Hardcover ISBN: 978-0-39957804-5
eBook ISBN: 978-0-39957805-2

Printed in China

Design by Margaux Keres

10 9 8 7 6 5 4 3 2 1

First Edition